The Bhagavad Gita

The Bhagavad Gita is Hinduism's core sacred text, a dialogue of and on dharma. It enshrines the essential values of the Vedic, Upanishadic and epic traditions – *shruti* (the revealed) and *smriti* (the remembered). Its structure is informal question and answer; its mode is enquiry and search; its goal is self-discovery and spiritual illumination.

Purushottama Lal – poet, critic, transcreator of Sanskrit, Hindu, Bengali and Punjabi texts – is Professor of English at St. Xavier's College, Calcutta, since 1953. The recipient of the Padma Shri in 1970, he was also honoured with a D. Litt. by Westminster College in 1977.

The Bhagavad Gita

TRANSCREATED FROM SANSKRIT BY

P. Lal

LOTUS COLLECTION
ROLI BOOKS

Lotus Collection

For Kewlian Sio
sangavarjitah nirvairah yah
'who is free from desire and unaffected by anger'

First paperback edition 2004

Second impression 2005
The Lotus Collection
An imprint of
Roli Books Pvt. Ltd.
M-75, G.K. II Market
New Delhi 110 048
Phones: ++91 (11) 2921 2271, 2921 2782
2921 0886, Fax: ++91 (11) 2921 7185
E-mail: roli@vsnl.com; Website: rolibooks.com
Also at
Bangalore, Varanasi, Jaipur and the Netherlands

Published under arrangement with Writers Workshop

Cover design: Sneha Pamneja
Cover photo: Courtesy Martand Singh, Rta Kapur Chishti and Rahul Jain, from
their book 'Handcrafted Indian Textiles'.

Typeset in Galliard by Roli Books Pvt. Ltd. and
printed at Gopsons Papers Limited, New Delhi.

'Mahatma Gandhi treated the *Gita* as his "mother", for it is the core of the philosophy of unarmed resistance, even at the risk of losing one's life. Satyagraha, after all, is "soul-force". Those who take up the sword, warned Jesus, shall perish by it; but does it follow that those who die swordless in battle shall find life everlasting?

'Arjuna prefers to be the world's first pacifist, a conscientiously objecting, bravely quaking and Quaker Hindu. To call him a "coward", as Krishna does is an injustice. It requires a very special kind of courage to be "cowardly" in the Arjuna manner. Arjuna stands for ahimsa, Krishna recommends killing; Arjuna is the humanist, and Krishna is the militarist. And there is no reconciliation between these two fearfully opposed philosophies.'

' I love such devotees, is what Krishna is saying. A stage has now been reached in the relationship between confused Arjuna and confident Krishna when their Nara-Narayana closeness asserts itself. . . . Arjuna is Krishna's "sakha" (loving friend and loved friend); and now Arjuna is on the brink of becoming a "sakha-bhakta" (loved and loving friend-cum-devotee).

' It is to such a loving devotee that Krishna now offers insights into two of the subtlest concepts of Upanishadic philosophy: Purusha and Prakriti (Male and Female, or Soul and Matter) and Kshetra and Kshetrajna (Field and Knower of the Field). Both concepts are linked, and no spiritual aspirant can progress without a clear awareness of their meanings and implications. This is the knowledge that must be known. '

CONTENTS

INTRODUCTION

$\mathbf{I}$n a short preface to the first
edition of my English version of the *Bhagavad Gita* (published
by Writers Workshop in 1965) I wrote:

'I first translated the *Gita* in 1947, in rhymed English verse.
It was an adolescent experiment and, though a couplet or
two may not have sounded too bad, the iambs and anapaests
in general appeared to be contrived, precious, and terribly
archaic.

'Another attempt in prose, five years later, became too flat.
The original has the dignity and memorability of a chanted
poem. Prose is too thin a medium for it.

'The essential structure of the *Gita*, however, is question-
and-answer. Arjuna questions; Krishna answers. The tone is lofty,
but *intimate*; highly serious, but *friendly*; sacred, but colloquially
so. The present translation tries to preserve the dialogue spirit
of the Sanskrit, a spirit marked by simplicity, grace, brevity, and
clarity. I have tried to retain the *Gita's* sweetness of persuasion
and strength of conviction.

'Readers who discover in my version a certain dramatic
quality will be right in inferring that I see the sacred text of
Hinduism as an integral part of Vyasa's epic of India. In the epic,

the *Gita* appears to have only one purpose: to get Arjuna to fight. It is fitted neatly into the grand design of *dharmakshetra Kurukshetra*.'

A revised edition appeared in 1968, but I was not entirely satisfied with either version. Arjuna's behaviour on the battlefield —his refusal to fight and kill his relatives —inspired and simultaneously baffled me. It seemed to be out of character. Why should a Kshatriya hesitate to do his military duty? I felt the answer must lie in the *totality* of Arjuna's character, and to discover that totality I embarked on a major project: to transcreate the *Mahabharata* shloka by shloka, hoping in the process to find at least a few clues to clarify at least one of what I consider to be the three focal controversy-points in the *Gita*.

Twenty years and one hundred and fifty transcreated fascicules later, I have a few glimmerings, but still not the complete answer (assuming that there *is* a complete answer). Arjuna is a searching man, because he is troubled —unlike his brothers who are satisfied with conventional values. He is the only Pandava brother whose variety of erotic adventures suggests an almost restlessly twentieth-century hero seeking self-fulfillment through sexual satisfaction. He marries the princesses of Kalinga, Cedi, Madra, Magadha, and Yavana; in Hardwar he has a son Iravat by Ulupi, the Naga princess; in Manipura he marries Citrangada and has a son by her named Babhruvahana; in Dvaraka he abducts and marries Krishna's sister Subhadra and has a son by her, Abhimanyu. With the exception of Bhima (who marries the rakshasi Hidimba), the other Pandavas are happy with their common wife Draupadi. I suspect that Arjuna's mental make-up is worrying and questing, individualistic, even protestant. He cannot lose (because he possesses the invincible Gandiva bow), yet he will not fight. He prefers to be the world's first pacifist, a conscientiously objecting, bravely quaking and Quaker Hindu. To call him a 'coward', as Krishna does [II:3], is an injustice. It requires a very special kind of courage to be 'cowardly' in the Arjuna manner. For Arjuna stands for ahimsa, Krishna recommends killing; Arjuna in the *Gita* is, for whatever reason, the humanist, and Krishna, for whatever reason, is the militarist. And there is no reconciliation between these two fearfully opposed philosophies.

Which leads to the second focal point of debate in the *Gita* —I mean the nature of the Cosmic Revelation in Cantos X and XI. A careful reading of the *Gita* will show that Arjuna keeps on questioning and arguing with Krishna until Canto X. 'You bewilder me with confusing speech,' he says [III:2]. Quite naturally, for Krishna at one point comes up with a startling suggestion —the atman is eternal; only the body dies; so go ahead and kill —you will kill only the body, the atman will remain unaffected [II:19-21]. There could hardly be a better example of forked-tongue speciousness, and Arjuna is justified in asking if such dynamic 'action' is not worse than his passive non-doing based on 'knowledge' and conscience:

'If, as you say, Krishna, knowledge excels action,
Why do you urge me to this terrible war?' [III:1]

The truth of the matter surely is that no rational refutation is possible of the essential humanist position that killing is wrong, especially when such a stand is grounded in a clean conscience and is cleanly argued. Many of the answers given by Krishna appear to be evasive and occasionally not unsophistic. When logic fails, Krishna apparently resorts to divine magic, to maya. The *Gita* is transformed from a reasoning dialogue in Cantos I-IX to a poetical and mystical darshan in Cantos X-XI. Unable to satisfy a worried warrior's stricken conscience by rational argument, Krishna opts for the unusual —he stuns Arjuna with a glorious 'revelation' of psychedelic intensity. He succeeds; from Canto XII Arjuna accepts whatever Krishna has to offer. Brain is overpowered by bhakti —but is it ethical to silence logic with magic? It seems to me that Krishna employs a confidence trick and, being Divinity, he not only gets away with it but actually is praised in some quarters for providing a climactic mystic vision. What I mean is that, in the twentieth century, in the contemporary world, apocalyptically threatened by the unchecked proliferation of nuclear mushrooms, Arjuna stands for the voice of invincible conscience; he is the humanist hero who has risen above the demands of military caste and convention-ridden community. His plight on the field of Kurukshetra is not an abstract, condemnable intellectual perplexity that can be juggled away by a 'Cosmic Multi-Revelation'. It is a painful and honest problem that Krishna should have faced on its own terms, painfully and honestly, and did not. Or so the modern unimpressed mind thinks.

The third and last moral and religious insight —there are many others, but these three I consider to be the most stimulating and relevant in our age —comes in Canto XV. Krishna describes a 'cosmic fig-tree' whose roots are in the sky, whose fruits are on earth. 'Slice this fig-tree with non-attachment', he advises Arjuna, thus ending your karma and obtaining moksha. The co-ordinates of moksha are not given, because freedom, if truly free, can have no limiting co-ordinates, no how-to-achieve-it gimmickry.

This cosmic fig-tree is a metaphor for one of Hinduism's profoundest and subtlest beliefs, a metaphor that has found its way into Indian village folklore as the *kalpa-taru*, the Wish-Fulfilling Tree. The Bengali folk singer Ram Prosad Sen has a song in which he says: 'Let's go, my mind, and pluck the four fruits.' These are the fruits that hang from the Wish-Fulfilling Tree. Christopher Isherwood retells the parable in his anthology *Vedanta for the West*; I narrated it in my introductory essay 'On Understanding India' to Barbara Harrison's *Learning About India* (1977). It is worth repeating, for it helps to make Krishna's point in the *Gita* clear. The story is exquisitely simple.

The proverbial benevolent uncle turns up in a village and finds his nephews and nieces and their friends playing in a hut with toys and make-do twig-and-rag dolls. 'Why play with these?' he asks. 'Outside is the *kalpa-taru*, the Wish-Fulfilling Tree. Stand under it, and wish. It will give you anything you want.'

The children don't believe him. They know the world's not structured to give you whatever you want. You have to struggle very hard for the smallest reward —and, of course, others always seem to get the plums, for they have what is known as 'connections.'

They smile knowingly. The uncle leaves.

No sooner has he left, however, than they rush to the Tree, and start wishing. They want sweets —and they get stomach ache. They want toys —and they get boredom. Bigger and better toys —bigger and better boredom.

This worries them. Something must be wrong somewhere. Someone is tricking them. What is this unpleasant unsuspected unwanted extra that tags along with the sweets and the toys?

What they have not realized yet is that the Wish-Fulfilling Tree is the enormously generous but totally unsentimental cosmos. It will give you exactly what you want —'this world is your wish-fulfilling cow,' says Krishna [III:10] —and with it its built-in opposite. Nothing in this world comes single; everything comes with its built-in opposite. The tragedy of the world is not that we don't get what we want, but that we always get exactly what we want —along with its built-in opposite. Wish it, think it, dream it, do it —you've got it! — and, literally, you've had it. That's it —having and being had.

So the children grow up and become, euphemistically, 'young adults.' They really are just a bunch of over-grown kids, all trapped under the Wishing Tree. Instead of sweets and toys —childish trifles! —they now crave Sex, Fame, Money, and Power, the four sweet fruits that hang from the tree. Bittersweet fruits. There are, truly speaking, no other fruits. There is nothing else to be had.

They reach out and bite each of these four fruits and get the same bitter after-taste of disappointment and disillusionment. But they go on wishing, because there seems to be little else that one can do under the Wishing Tree. Creatures come and go; the Tree is always there.

Then they grow old, and are stretched out under the tree, lying on their death cots. Pathetic old men and women, kindly referred to as 'guru-jana', 'respected elders'. They lie huddled in three security-seeking groups. The first group whispers, 'It's all a hoax. The world's a farce.' Fools; they have learnt nothing.

The second huddle whispers, 'We made the wrong wishes. We'll wish again. This time we'll make the right wish.' Bigger fools; they have learnt less than nothing.

The third group is the most foolish. 'What's the point living? Nothing makes sense. We want to die.'

The obliging tree quickly grants their last desire. They die

—and they get the built-in opposite of the death-wish —they are re-born —and under the same tree, for there is no other place to get born or re-born in.

The parable does not end here. It speaks of a lame boy. The young cripple also hobbled to the tree, but was shoved aside by his more agile friends. So he crawled back to the hut and gazed at the marvellous tree from the window, waiting for a chance for him to go and make the wish that lame boys make. What he saw from the window awed and almost unnerved him.

He saw his companions wanting sweets and getting stomach ache, grabbing toys and getting bored. He saw them scrambling for Sex, Fame, Money, and Power, and getting their opposites, and agonizing —and not realizing the cause of their anguish. He saw them divided into three groups —the Cynics, the self-appointed Wise Guys, and the hope-bereft Death-wishers. He saw this clearly, with the poignant brilliant sharpness of naked truth.

The spectacle of this cosmic swindle so *impressed* him that he stood stunned in brief, lucid bafflement. A divine comedy, a divine tragicomedy, the panoramic cycle of karma, was being enacted in front of his eyes. A gush of compassion welled in his heart for the victims of karma, and in that gush of compassion the lame boy forgot to wish. He had sliced the cosmic fig-tree with non-attachment.

He stood outside the orbit of the world's ambivalence.

He had, in showing spontaneous compassion, not done the planned good act, which earns heaven for its doer and leads to better rebirth. The Hindu heaven is a temporary state, because heaven is really a punishment for good deeds.

Nor had he done the 'bad' act, which earns hell, again temporary, after which one is born again. The Hindu tradition feels that no crime is so bad as to deserve an eternity of punishment.

He had not done the absurd act, either, by opting to cop out of the system. After all, my life is my life, and I can take it whenever I want to; there's no one really to stop me.

He had sliced the cosmic fig-tree by doing the 'pure' act, the act of gratuitous compassion, which gets no reward or punishment, since it lies outside the give-and-take orbit. The pure act —nishkama karma —is its own reward. Until the gesture of the pure act is made, we are all trapped under the Wish-Fulfilling Tree. The cripple did not *consciously* know this. He stood, in the medicinal shade of his compassion and beyond the pale of the Tree, marvelling at the wondrous and complex and dread fabric of the universe, and forgetting to wish. Forgetting, not remembering to forget. He was the 'free', the serene man, the genuine candidate for moksha, untouched by the world's ambivalence, and by the heaven and hell the world so copiously offers.

The big question is: Is such compassion possible? Krishna says, 'Act one *must* —the body compels it —true giving-up is renunciation of fruits' [XVIII:2]. Yes, but can the ordinary human being ever give up the fruits of action? Is the carrot dangled by Krishna ever achievable through the ego-ridden efforts of mankind? Is Hinduism again talking so big and positing goals so idealistic that, with the exception of saints, all must despair of success? Is it reasonable, is it practical to expect Arjuna, trained as a Kshatriya, expert in the arts of war, to fight without desire to win?

Calcutta   *P. Lal*
June 1994

ARJUNA'S GRIEF

*B*ecause *Arjuna refuses to act — he won't fight his friends, relatives, and gurus — the epic story of the* Mahabharata *slides to a standstill. Without action, no narrative is possible; indeed, no life. Krishna in the* Gita *provides the kick start by stressing the imperative need to act. Very simply, the* Gita *is a compressed analysis of the three kinds of action possible in human affairs: ritual action (for the physically inclined), reasoned action (for the intellectual), and spiritual action (for those inspired by religious devotion).*

The key shloka of Canto 1 is the last (47). Arjuna, stricken by paralyzing sorrow, swirling in indecision's quicksand, throws away his bow and quiver, and slumps down on his war-chariot.

He gives three reasons for his suddenly discovered 'pacifism'. One: sva-jana (one's own people) are to be respected and loved, not 'wasted'. Two: others, blinded by greed, may go in for kula-kshaya (family ruin), but mutually assured destruction is not the civilized way of responding to aggression; certainly not his way. Three: killing is the ultimate crime; better to be killed weaponless (ashastram) than kill, whatever the context of contention.

No wonder Mahatma Gandhi treated the Gita *as his 'mother', for here is the core of the philosophy of unarmed resistance, even at the risk of losing one's life. Satyagraha, after all, is 'soul-force'. Those who take up the sword, warned Jesus, shall perish by it; but does it follow that those who die swordless in battle shall find life everlasting?*

धृतराष्ट्र उवाच

धर्मक्षेत्रे कुरुक्षेत्रे समवेता युयुत्सवः ।
मामकाः पाण्डवाश्चैव किमकुर्वत सञ्जय ॥ १ ॥

सञ्जय उवाच

दृष्ट्वा तु पाण्डवानीकं व्यूढं दुर्योधनस्तदा ।
आचार्यमुपसङ्गम्य राजा वचनमब्रवीत् ॥ २ ॥

पश्यैतां पाण्डुपुत्राणामाचार्य महतीं चमूम् ।
व्यूढां द्रुपदपुत्रेण तव शिष्येण धीमता ॥ ३ ॥

अत्र शूरा महेष्वासा भीमार्जुनसमा युधि ।
युयुधानो विराटश्च द्रुपदश्च महारथः ॥ ४ ॥

धृष्टकेतुश्चेकितानः काशिराजश्च वीर्यवान् ।
पुरुजित्कुन्तिभोजश्च शैब्यश्च नरपुङ्गवः ॥ ५ ॥

युधामन्युश्च विक्रान्त उत्तमौजाश्च वीर्यवान् ।
सौभद्रो द्रौपदेयाश्च सर्व एव महारथाः ॥ ६ ॥

अस्माकं तु विशिष्टा ये तान्निबोध द्विजोत्तम ।
नायका मम सैन्यस्य संज्ञार्थं तान्ब्रवीमि ते ॥ ७ ॥

भवान्भीष्मश्च कर्णश्च कृपश्च समितिंजयः ।
अश्वत्थामा विकर्णश्च सौमदत्तिस्तथैव च ॥ ८ ॥

अन्ये च बहवः शूरा मदर्थे त्यक्तजीविताः ।
नानाशस्त्रप्रहरणाः सर्वे युद्धविशारदाः ॥ ९ ॥

अपर्याप्तं तदस्माकं बलं भीष्माभिरक्षितम् ।
पर्याप्तं त्विदमेतेषां बलं भीमाभिरक्षितम् ॥ १० ॥

अयनेषु च सर्वेषु यथाभागमवस्थिताः ।
भीष्ममेवाभिरक्षन्तु भवन्तः सर्व एव हि ॥ ११ ॥

तस्य संजनयन्हर्षं कुरुवृद्धः पितामहः ।
सिंहनादं विनद्योच्चैः शङ्खं दध्मौ प्रतापवान् ॥ १२ ॥

1   Dhritarashtra asked:
Tell me, Sanjaya,
What did the Pandavas and Kauravas do,
    gathered on the sacred battlefield of Kurukshetra?

2   Sanjaya replied:
Seeing the army of the Pandavas,
Duryodhana went to his acharya Drona, and said:

3   'Look at the vast army of the Pandavas,
under the command of Dhrishtadyumna:

4   Heroes all of them, mighty bowmen rivalling Bhima and
    Arjuna:
Yuyudhana, Virata, and Drupada,

5   Dhrishtaketu, Chekitana and the king of Varanasi,
Purujit, Kuntibhoja, and Shaibya:

6   Yudhamanyu, and Uttamaujas,
Abhimanyu and the sons and grandsons of Drupada.

7   And look at your army too, O Brahmin;
I give you the names of our commanders:

8   First of all, you, Bhishma, Karna, and Kripa:
Ashvatthaman, Vikarna, and the son of Somadatta:

9   And many others, all well-armed,
eager to die if necessary for my sake.

10 My army seems weak compared to theirs,
mine marshalled by Bhishma, theirs by Bhima.

11 Let orders be passed to protect Bhishma:
let the troops form ranks.'

12 Bhishma, anxious to revive Duryodhana's spirits,
blew fiercely on his conch, like a lion roaring.

ततः शङ्खाश्च भेर्यश्च पणवानकगोमुखाः ।
सहसैवाभ्यहन्यन्त स शब्दस्तुमुलोऽभवत् ॥ १३ ॥

ततः श्वेतैर्हयैर्युक्ते महति स्यन्दने स्थितौ ।
माधवः पाण्डवश्चैव दिव्यौ शङ्खौ प्रदध्मतुः ॥ १४ ॥

पाञ्चजन्यं हृषीकेशो देवदत्तं धनञ्जयः ।
पौण्ड्रं दध्मौ महाशङ्खं भीमकर्मा वृकोदरः ॥ १५ ॥

अनन्तविजयं राजा कुन्तीपुत्रो युधिष्ठिरः ।
नकुलः सहदेवश्च सुघोषमणिपुष्पकौ ॥ १६ ॥

काश्यश्च परमेष्वासः शिखण्डी च महारथः ।
धृष्टद्युम्नो विराटश्च सात्यकिश्चापराजितः ॥ १७ ॥

द्रुपदो द्रौपदेयाश्च सर्वशः पृथिवीपते ।
सौभद्रश्च महाबाहुः शङ्खान्दध्मुः पृथक्पृथक् ॥ १८ ॥

स घोषो धार्तराष्ट्राणां हृदयानि व्यदारयत् ।
नभश्च पृथिवीं चैव तुमुलो व्यनुनादयन् ॥ १९ ॥

अथ व्यवस्थितान्दृष्ट्वा धार्तराष्ट्रान् कपिध्वजः ।
प्रवृत्ते शस्त्रसंपाते धनुरुद्यम्य पाण्डवः ॥ २० ॥

हृषीकेशं तदा वाक्यमिदमाह महीपत ।

अर्जुन उवाच

सेनयोरुभयोर्मध्ये रथं स्थापय मेऽच्युत ॥ २१ ॥

यावदेतान्निरीक्षेऽहं योद्धुकामानवस्थितान् ।
कैर्मया सह योद्धव्यमस्मिन्नंणसमुद्यमे ॥ २२ ॥

योत्स्यमानानवेक्षेऽहं य एतेऽत्र समागताः ।
धार्तराष्ट्रस्य दुर्बुद्धेर्युद्धे प्रियचिकीर्षवः ॥ २३ ॥

सञ्जय उवाच

एवमुक्तो हृषीकेशो गुडाकेशेन भारत ।
सेनयोरुभयोर्मध्ये स्थापयित्वा रथोत्तमम् ॥ २४ ॥

13   Conches, kettledrums, horns and tabors blew suddenly.
      The noise was tremendous.

14   Standing in their white-horsed chariot,
      Krishna and Arjuna blew their conches.

15   Krishna's conch was called Panchajanya,
      Arjuna's Devadatta, and Bhima's Paundra.

16   And Yudhishthira blew his conch of Endless Victory,
      Nakula his of Honey Tone, and Sahadeva his called the
         Jewel Blossom.

17   Each blew his own conch —the supreme archer,
         the king of Varanasi, the mighty charioteer Shikhandin,
      Dhrishtadyumna, Virata and the undefeated Satyaki;

18   Drupada, too, and Draupadi's sons,
      and the strong-muscled Abhimanyu.

19   And thunderous peal after peal, crashing through heaven
         and earth,
      shattered the morale of Dhritarashtra's camp.

20   Seeing Dhritarashtra's men eager for war, and battle
         impending,
      ape-emblemed Arjuna lifted his bow and turned to Krishna.

21   Arjuna said to Krishna:
      'Take my chariot, Krishna,
      between the two camps:

22   Let me see my enemy before I fight him.
      Who are the ones gathered here for bloodshed?

23   I can see them,
      flatterers of evil Duryodhana on sacred Kurukshetra.'

24   On Arjuna's request,
      Krishna took the glittering chariot midfield.

भीष्मद्रोणप्रमुखतः सर्वेषां च महीक्षिताम् ।
उवाच पार्थ पश्यैतान् समवेतान्कुरूनिति ॥ २५ ॥

तत्रापश्यत्स्थितान्पार्थः पितॄनथ पितामहान् ।
आचार्यान्मातुलान्भ्रातॄन्पुत्रान्पौत्रान्सखींस्तथा ॥ २६ ॥

श्वशुरान्सुहृदश्चैव सेनयोरूभयोरपि ।
तान्समीक्ष्य स कौन्तेयः सर्वान्बन्धूनवस्थितान् ॥ २७ ॥

कृपया परयाविष्टो विषीदन्निदमब्रवीत् ।

अर्जुन उवाच

दृष्ट्वेमं स्वजनं कृष्ण युयुत्सुं समुपस्थितम् ॥ २८ ॥

सीदन्ति मम गात्राणि मुखं च परिशुष्यति ।
वेपथुश्च शरीरे मे रोमहर्षश्च जायते ॥ २९ ॥

गाण्डीवं स्रंसते हस्तात्त्वक्चैव परिदह्यते ।
न च शक्नोम्यवस्थातुं भ्रमतीव च मे मनः ॥ ३० ॥

निमित्तानि च पश्यामि विपरीतानि केशव ।
न च श्रेयोऽनुपश्यामि हत्वा स्वजनमाहवे ॥ ३१ ॥

न काङ्क्षे विजयं कृष्ण न च राज्यं सुखानि च ।
किं नो राज्येन गोविन्द किं भोगैर्जीवितेन वा ॥ ३२ ॥

येषामर्थे काङ्क्षितं नो राज्यं भोगाः सुखानि च ।
त इमेऽवस्थिता युद्धे प्राणांस्त्यक्त्वा धनानि च ॥ ३३ ॥

आचार्याः पितरः पुत्रास्तथैव च पितामहाः ।
मातुलाः श्वशुराः पौत्राः श्यालाः सम्बन्धिनस्तथा ॥ ३४ ॥

एतान्न हन्तुमिच्छामि घ्नतोऽपि मधुसूदन ।
अपि त्रैलोक्यराज्यस्य हेतोः किं नु महीकृते ॥ ३५ ॥

निहत्य धार्तराष्ट्रान्नः का प्रीतिः स्याज्जनार्दन ।
पापमेवाश्रयेदस्मान्हत्वैतानाततायिनः ॥ ३६ ॥

25   Facing Bhishma, Drona and the lords of the Earth, he said:
      'Here are the Kauravas, Arjuna.'

26   Arjuna saw, in the camps of both,
          his fathers and grandfathers, his brothers and cousins,
      his sons and grandsons, his friends and acharyas,

27   His fathers-in-law and acquaintances.
      He saw his kinsmen assembled for war.

28   Arjuna, stirred to compassion, said:
      I have seen my kinsmen gathered for war;

29   My mouth is dry with fear,
      my limbs refuse to listen to me, trembling seizes me;

30   My skin chafes, and the divine Gandiva bow slips from
          my hand.
      Neither can I stand erect: my mind whirls,

31   And unholy omens appear before my eyes.
      In killing my brothers, Krishna,
          I cannot see anything noble —

32   I do not want this victory, this glory, this happiness.
      What is glory to us, Krishna, what are pleasures and life,

33   If those who from us deserve glory, pleasure, and life,
      are ready to fight us, having given up the world's delights —

34   Our uncles, our sons and our grandfathers,
      our eldest kinsmen, acharyas, our fathers-in-law and our
          grandsons.

35   I would not kill them, not for the three worlds, let alone
          the earth.
      I had rather they killed me, Krishna.

36   What joy is there in slaying Dhritarashtra's sons? —
      It is a terrible crime to kill them, however much we hate them.

तस्मान्नार्हा वयं हन्तुं धार्तराष्ट्रान् स्वबान्धवान् ।
स्वजनं हि कथं हत्वा सुखिनः स्याम माधवः ॥ ३७ ॥

यद्यप्येते न पश्यन्ति लोभोपहतचेतसः ।
कुलक्षयकृतं दोषं मित्रद्रोहे च पातकम् ॥ ३८ ॥

कथं न ज्ञेयमस्माभिः पापादस्मान्निवर्तितुम् ।
कुलक्षयकृतं दोषं प्रपश्यद्भिर्जनार्दन ॥ ३९ ॥

कुलक्षये प्रणश्यन्ति कुलधर्माः सनातनाः ।
धर्मे नष्टे कुलं कृत्स्नमधर्मोऽभिभवत्युत ॥ ४० ॥

अधर्माभिभवात्कृष्ण प्रदुष्यन्ति कुलस्त्रियः ।
स्त्रीषु दुष्टासु वार्ष्णेय जायते वर्णसङ्करः ॥ ४१ ॥

सङ्करो नरकायैव कुलघ्नानां कुलस्य च ।
पतन्ति पितरो ह्येषां लुप्तपिण्डोदकक्रियाः ॥ ४२ ॥

दोषैरेतैः कुलघ्नानां वर्णसङ्करकारकैः ।
उत्साद्यन्ते जातिधर्माः कुलधर्माश्च शाश्वताः ॥ ४३ ॥

उत्सन्नकुलधर्माणां मनुष्याणां जनार्दन ।
नरकेऽनियतं वासो भवतीत्यनुशुश्रुम ॥ ४४ ॥

अहो बत महत्पापं कर्तुं व्यवसिता वयम् ।
यद्राज्यसुखलोभेन हन्तुं स्वजनमुद्यताः ॥ ४५ ॥

यदि मामप्रतीकारमशस्त्रं शस्त्रपाणयः ।
धार्तराष्ट्रा रणे हन्युस्तन्मे क्षेमतरं भवेत् ॥ ४६ ॥

सञ्जय उवाच

एवमुक्त्वार्जुनः संख्ये रथोपस्थ उपाविशत् ।
विसृज्य सशरं चापं शोकसंविग्नमानसः ॥ ४७ ॥

37   I will not kill my kinsmen, Krishna:
     how could happiness be mine if I murder my brothers?

38   Their reason obscured by greed,
     they see no wrong in disunion of brothers, in hate
          against friends;

39   But we, the clear of mind who understand right and wrong,
     should we not refrain from such vile acts?

40   Family dharma disappears in the family when the family
          breaks up;
     that disappearing, adharma takes over.

41   Where adharma rules, the women are corrupted;
     with the women corrupted, even caste is endangered.

42   Intermixture of castes spells of doom for the family; as
          well as for the destroyers of the family;
     the spirits of the ancestors fall, denied rice-and-water homage.

43   And by this looseness of the destroyers of the family
     is the age-old dharma of caste and the family destroyed.

44   We have heard, Krishna,
     hell awaits the families which discard dharma.

45   Aho!
     What a terrible thing it is to kill brothers, and cast
          covetous eyes on their land!

46   Let the sons of Dhritarashtra kill me.
     I will not protest. Better be killed than kill.

47   Sanjaya said:
     Arjuna flung away his bow and quiver,
     and slumped down on the seat of his glittering chariot,
          stricken with sorrow.

THE PATH OF YOGA

*T*he third shloka of Canto II is its key: 'Don't be a coward, Arjuna.' It is not ordinary debility; not disability; not inability that Arjuna suffers from. It's hridya-durbala (heart-non-strength). This, in psychological terms, is indecisiveness resulting from confusion and an erroneous sense of insecurity. In spiritual terminology, it is a moral paralysis of the will caused by fear of death or, indeed, by dread of the pointlessness of life itself.

But how to overcome this fearful fear of fear? Krishna provides many clues, but it is Arjuna who wraps them all up by using, in shloka 54, what is one of the most popular and discussed compounds of the Gita: sthita-prajya (the steady-minded person). Nothing is possible if the mind is not steady, poised, balanced, tranquil, for only then can it do properly what it is programmed to do: think clearly. The steady-minded person cultivates restraint, selflessness, detachment. By allowing life to happen calmly to him instead of he happening to life passionately, he discovers and cherishes the truth that something higher than matter pervades matter and transcends matter. This something is the atman, the quintessential principle of life itself. If all matter disappeared, the atman would remain, because 'the untrue never is; the True never is not'. Matter is the perishable dress warn by the imperishable Spirit. This sthita-prajna realization must become the basis for Arjuna's commitment on the battlefield — and, indeed, for everyone's commitment in the complex business of daily living.

सञ्जय उवाच

तं तथा कृपयाविष्टमश्रुपूर्णाकुलेक्षणम् ।
विषीदन्तमिदं वाक्यमुवाच मधुसूदनः ॥ १ ॥

श्रीभगवानुवाच

कुतस्त्वा कश्मलमिदं विषमे समुपस्थितम् ।
अनार्यजुष्टमस्वर्ग्यमकीर्तिकरमर्जुन ॥ २ ॥

क्लैब्यं मा स्म गमः पार्थ नैतत्त्वय्युपपद्यते ।
क्षुद्रं हृदयदौर्बल्यं त्यक्त्वोत्तिष्ठ परंतप ॥ ३ ॥

अर्जुन उवाच

कथं भीष्ममहं संख्ये द्रोणं च मधुसूदन ।
इषुभिः प्रतियोत्स्यामि पूजार्हावरिसूदन ॥ ४ ॥

गुरूनहत्वा हि महानुभावान् श्रेयो भोक्तुं भैक्ष्यमपीह लोके ।
हत्वार्थकामांस्तु गुरूनिहैव भुञ्जीय भोगान् रुधिरप्रदिग्धान् ॥ ५ ॥

न चैतद्विद्मः कतरन्नो गरीयो यद्वा जयेम यदि वा नो जयेयुः ।
यानेव हत्वा न जिजीविषामस्तेऽवस्थिताः प्रमुखे धार्तराष्ट्राः ॥ ६ ॥

कार्पण्यदोषोपहतस्वभावः पृच्छामि त्वां धर्मसंमूढचेताः ।
यच्छ्रेयः स्यान्निश्चितं ब्रूहि तन्मे
शिष्यस्तेऽहं शाधि मां त्वां प्रपन्नम् ॥ ७ ॥

न हि प्रपश्यामि ममापनुद्याद्
यच्छोकमुच्छोषणमिन्द्रियाणाम् ।
अवाप्य भूमावसपत्नमृद्धं राज्यं सुराणामपि चाधिपत्यम् ॥ ८ ॥

सञ्जय उवाच

एवमुक्त्वा हृषीकेशं गुडाकेशः परंतप ।
न योत्स्य इति गोविन्दमुक्त्वा तूष्णीं बभूव ह ॥ ९ ॥

तमुवाच हृषीकेशः प्रहसन्निव भारत ।
सेनयोरुभयोर्मध्ये विषीदन्तमिदं वचः ॥ १० ॥

1   Sanjaya reported:
Krishna's words to Arjuna, whose mind was heavy with grief
and whose eyes were filled with tears of pity, were:

2   Your sorrow in this crisis, Arjuna, is disgraceful.
It stands in the way of heavenly fulfilment.

3   Don't be a coward, Arjuna.
It does not become you at all. Shake off your weakness and
rise!

4   Arjuna replied:
How can I fight Bhishma and Drona, my gurus,
who deserve my veneration?

5   Why, it would be preferable to live as a beggar than kill these
great gurus.
To murder teachers is to eat blood-stained food.

6   Who can say which is better, Krishna, we defeating them or
they defeating us?
Dhritarashtra's *sons* are our enemies. Killing them will bring
us life-long misery.

7   Paralyzed by pity, full of doubts, I ask for your grace.
I am your worshipper. Put me on the right path. Show me
what is good for me.

8   I know of nothing that can remove this sense-killing
sorrow —
neither tyranny over the gods nor kingship of the earth.

9   Sanjaya continued:
These were Arjuna's words to Krishna.
He added, 'I will not fight,' and lapsed into silence.

10 To Arjuna, sad in the middle of the battlefield,
Krishna, as if smiling, said:

श्रीभगवानुवाच

अशोच्यानन्वशोचस्त्वं प्रज्ञावादांश्च भाषसे ।
गतासूनगतासूंश्च नानुशोचन्ति पण्डिताः ॥ ११ ॥

न त्वेवाहं जातु नासं न त्वं नेमे जनाधिपाः ।
न चैव न भविष्यामः सर्वे वयमतः परम् ॥ १२ ॥

देहिनोऽस्मिन्यथा देहे कौमारं यौवनं जरा ।
तथा देहान्तरप्राप्तिर्धीरस्तत्र न मुह्यति ॥ १३ ॥

मात्रास्पर्शास्तु कौन्तेय शीतोष्णसुखदुःखदाः ।
आगमापायिनोऽनित्यास्तांस्तितिक्षस्व भारत ॥ १४ ॥

यं हि न व्यथयन्त्येते पुरुषं पुरुषर्षभ ।
समदुःखसुखं धीरं सोऽमृतत्वाय कल्पते ॥ १५ ॥

नासतो विद्यते भावो नाभावो विद्यते सतः ।
उभयोरपि दृष्टोऽन्तस्त्वनयोस्तत्त्वदर्शिभिः ॥ १६ ॥

अविनाशि तु तद्विद्धि येन सर्वमिदं ततम् ।
विनाशमव्ययस्यास्य न कश्चित्कर्तुमर्हति ॥ १७ ॥

अन्तवन्त इमे देहा नित्यस्योक्ताः शरीरिणः ।
अनाशिनोऽप्रमेयस्य तस्माद्युध्यस्व भारत ॥ १८ ॥

य एनं वेत्ति हन्तारं यश्चैनं मन्यते हतम् ।
उभौ तौ न विजानीतो नायं हन्ति न हन्यते ॥ १९ ॥

न जायते म्रियते वा कदाचि-
　　　　नायं भूत्वा भविता वा न भूयः ।
अजो नित्यः शाश्वतोऽयं पुराणो
　　　　न हन्यते हन्यमाने शरीरे ॥ २० ॥

11   You mourn those, Arjuna, who do not deserve mourning.
      The learned mourn neither the living nor the dead.
          (Your words only sound wise).

12   Do not think that I never was. that you are not, that all
          these kings are not.
      And it was not that we shall cease to be in the future.

13   To the embodied atman childhood, maturity and old age
          happen naturally.
      The acquisition of a new body is natural too. This does not
          confuse the steady soul.

14   Heat, cold, pain, pleasure —these spring from sensual contact,
          Arjuna.
      They begin, and they end. They exist for the time being.
          Endure them.

15   The man whom these cannot distract, the man who is steady
          in pain and pleasure,
      is the man who achieves serenity.

16   The untrue never is; the True never is not.
      The knowers of truth know this.

17   And the Self that pervades all things is imperishable.
      Nothing corrupts this imperishable Self.

18   How utterly strange that bodies are said to be destroyed when
          the immutable, illimitable and indestructible Self lives on!
      Therefore, rise, Arjuna, and fight!

19   Who sees the Self as slayer, and who sees it as slain, know
          nothing about the Self.
      This does not slay. It is not slain.

20   It is not born, it does not die. It does not evolve.
      It is birthless, changeless, and eternal. It does not die when
          the body dies.

वेदाविनाशिनं नित्यं य एनमजमव्ययम् ।
कथं स पुरूषः पार्थ कं घातयति हन्ति कम् ॥ २१ ॥

वासांसि जीर्णानि यथा विहाय
      नवानि गृह्णाति नरोऽपराणि ।
तथा शरीराणि विहाय जीर्णा-
      न्यन्यानि संयाति नवानि देही ॥ २२ ॥

नैनं छिन्दन्ति शस्त्राणि नैनं दहति पावकः ।
न चैनं क्लेदयन्त्यापो न शोषयति मारुतः ॥ २३ ॥

अच्छेद्योऽयमदाह्योऽयमक्लेद्योऽशोष्य एव च ।
नित्यः सर्वगतः स्थाणुरचलोऽयं सनातनः ॥ २४ ॥

अव्यक्तोऽयमचिन्त्योऽयमविकार्योऽयमुच्यते ।
तस्मादेवं विदित्वैनं नानुशोचितुमर्हसि ॥ २५ ॥

अथ चैनं नित्यजातं नित्यं वा मन्यसे मृतम् ।
तथापि त्वं महाबाहो नैवं शोचितुमर्हसि ॥ २६ ॥

जातस्य हि ध्रुवो मृत्युर्ध्रुवं जन्म मृतस्य च ।
तस्मादपरिहार्येऽर्थे न त्वं शोचितुमर्हसि ॥ २७ ॥

अव्यक्तादीनि भूतानि व्यक्तमध्यानि भारत ।
अव्यक्तनिधनान्येव तत्र का परिदेवना ॥ २८ ॥

आश्चर्यवत्पश्यति कश्चिदेन-
      माश्चर्यवद्वदति तथैव चान्यः ।
आश्चर्यवच्चैनमन्यः शृणोति
      श्रुत्वाप्येनं वेद न चैव कश्चित् ॥ २९ ॥

देही नित्यमवध्योऽयं देहे सर्वस्य भारत ।
तस्मात्सर्वाणि भूतानि न त्वं शोचितुमर्हसि ॥ ३० ॥

स्वधर्ममपि चावेक्ष्य न विकम्पितुमर्हसि ।
धर्म्याद्धि युद्धाच्छ्रेयोऽन्यत्क्षत्रियस्य न विद्यते ॥ ३१ ॥

21   And if a man knows it as imperishable, changeless, and
          birthless,
       how can he possibly kill, or make another kill?

22   As a person throws away worn-out clothes and puts on a new
          dress,
       the embodied Self throws away the worn-out body and enters
       a new one.

23   Weapons do not harm this Self, fire does not burn it,
       water does not wet it, wind does not dry it.

24   It cannot be cut, kindled, wetted, dried;
       immobile, immovable, immutable, all-pervasive, it is eternal.

25   It is unmanifest, unknowable, and unchangeable.
       Realize this, and do not grieve.

26   Even if it were endlessly to be born,
       and endlessly to die, you should not grieve.

27   For death is sure of that which is born, and of that which
          is dead, birth is certain.
       Why do you grieve over the inevitable?

28   All beings are unmanifest in the beginning, manifest in the
          middle, and again unmanifest at the end.
       Is this a cause for grief?

29   It's wonderful to see it, wonderful to hear about it,
          wonderful to talk about it.
       But it's impossible to know it.

30   This embodied atman, Arjuna, is imperishable.
       You have no reason to grieve for any creature.

31   Think of your own dharma, and do not hesitate, for
       there is nothing greater to a warrior than a just war.

यदृच्छया चोपपन्नं स्वर्गद्वारमपावृतम् ।
सुखिनः क्षत्रियाः पार्थ लभन्ते युद्धमीदृशम् ॥ ३२ ॥

अथ चेत्त्वमिमं धर्म्यं संग्रामं न करिष्यसि ।
ततः स्वधर्मं कीर्तिं च हित्वा पापमवाप्स्यसि ॥ ३३ ॥

अकीर्तिं चापि भूतानि
            कथयिष्यन्ति तेऽव्ययाम् ।
सम्भावितस्य चाकीर्ति-
            र्मरणादतिरिच्यते ॥ ३४ ॥

भयाद्रणादुपरतं मंस्यन्ते त्वां महारथाः ।
येषां च त्वं बहुमतो भूत्वा यास्यसि लाघवम् ॥ ३५ ॥

अवाच्यवादांश्च बहून्वदिष्यन्ति तवाहिताः ।
निन्दन्तस्तव सामर्थ्यं ततो दुःखतरं नु किम् ॥ ३६ ॥

हतो वा प्राप्स्यसि स्वर्गं जित्वा वा भोक्ष्यसे महीम् ।
तस्मादुत्तिष्ठ कौन्तेय युद्धाय कृतनिश्चयः ॥ ३७ ॥

सुखदुःखे समे कृत्वा लाभालाभौ जयाजयौ ।
ततो युद्धाय युज्यस्व नैवं पापमवाप्स्यसि ॥ ३८ ॥

एषा तेऽभिहिता सांख्ये
            बुद्धियोंगे त्विमां शृणु ।
बुद्ध्या युक्तो यया पार्थ
            कर्मबन्धं प्रहास्यसि ॥ ३९ ॥

नेहाभिक्रमनाशोऽस्ति प्रत्यवायो न विद्यते ।
स्वल्पमप्यस्य धर्मस्य त्रायते महतो भयात् ॥ ४० ॥

व्यवसायात्मिका बुद्धिरेकेह कुरुनन्दन ।
बहुशाखा ह्यनन्ताश्च बुद्धयोऽव्यवसायिनाम् ॥ ४१ ॥

यामिमां पुष्पितां वाचं प्रवदन्त्यविपश्चितः ।
वेदवादरताः पार्थ नान्यदस्तीति वादिनः ॥ ४२ ॥

कामात्मानः स्वर्गपरा जन्मकर्मफलप्रदाम् ।
क्रियाविशेषबहुलां भोगैश्वर्यगतिं प्रति ॥ ४३ ॥

32 Lucky are soldiers who fight in such a war;
    for them it is an easy entry into heaven.

33 But if you persist in ignoring dharma,
        your dignity and sva-dharma are lost;
    and you expose yourself to shame.

34 Your shame will never end.
    Shame is worse than death to a man of honour.

35 The chariot-warriors will say, 'He fled.'
    And those who once praised you will brand you a coward.

36 Your enemies will hurl insults at you.
    What could be more painful?

37 Die, and enjoy heaven. Live, and enjoy the world.
    Arise, Arjuna, and fight!

38 Equate pain and pleasure, profit and loss, victory and defeat.
    And fight! There is no blame this way.

39 I have given you the theory. Now listen to the practice.
    Learn how to break the fetters of karma.

40 There is no waste of half-done work in this and no going
        back.
    A little of this dharma removes a world of fear.

41 In this there is only single-minded will;
    while the efforts of confused people are many-branching
        and full of contradiction.

42 There is no constancy in the man who runs after pleasure
        and power,
    whose reason is robbed by the fool's flattery,

43 Who abiding by the rules of the Vedas
    proclaims that there is nothing else.

भोगैश्वर्यप्रसक्तानां तयापहृतचेतसाम् ।
व्यवसायात्मिका बुद्धिः समाधौ न विधीयते ॥ ४४ ॥

त्रैगुण्यविषया वेदा निस्त्रैगुण्यो भवार्जुन ।
निर्द्वन्द्वो नित्यसत्त्वस्थो निर्योगक्षेम आत्मवान् ॥ ४५ ॥

यावानर्थ उदपाने सर्वतः सम्प्लुतोदके ।
तावान्सर्वेषु वेदेषु ब्राह्मणस्य विजानतः ॥ ४६ ॥

कर्मण्येवाधिकारस्ते मा फलेषु कदाचन ।
मा कर्मफलहेतुर्भूर्मा ते सङ्गोऽस्त्वकर्मणि ॥ ४७ ॥

योगस्थः कुरु कर्माणि सङ्गं त्यक्त्वा धनञ्जय ।
सिद्ध्यसिद्ध्योः समो भूत्वा समत्वं योग उच्यते ॥ ४८ ॥

दूरेण ह्यवरं कर्म बुद्धियोगाद्धनञ्जय ।
बुद्धौ शरणमन्विच्छ कृपणाः फलहेतवः ॥ ४९ ॥

बुद्धियुक्तो जहातीह उभे सुकृतदुष्कृते ।
तस्माद्योगाय युज्यस्व योगः कर्मसु कौशलम् ॥ ५० ॥

कर्मजं बुद्धियुक्ता हि फलं त्यक्त्वा मनीषिणः ।
जन्मबन्धविनिर्मुक्ताः पदं गच्छन्त्यनामयम् ॥ ५१ ॥

यदा ते मोहकलिलं बुद्धिर्व्यतितरिष्यति ।
तदा गन्तासि निर्वेदं श्रोतव्यस्य श्रुतस्य च ॥ ५२ ॥

श्रुतिविप्रतिपन्ना ते यदा स्थास्यति निश्चला ।
समाधावचला बुद्धिस्तदा योगमवाप्स्यसि ॥ ५३ ॥

44   The honeyed rituals of the Vedas, promising enjoyment
          and power,
      are certain to lead him into fresh births.

45   The Vedas deal with three qualities.
      Know them, detach yourself from them, keep your poise,
          detach yourself from selfishness, and be firm in your Self.

46   The Vedas are as useless to a self-aware Brahmin
      as a pond when water has flooded the land.

47   Your duty is to work, not to reap the fruits of work.
      Do not seek rewards, but do not love laziness either.

48   Be steady in Yoga, do whatever you must do; give up
          attachment, be indifferent to failure and success.
      This stability is Yoga.

49   Selfish work is inferior to the work of a balanced,
          uncoveting mind; shelter yourself in this mental stability,
          Arjuna.
      Harassed are the seekers of the fruits of action.

50   With this mental poise you will release yourself from
          good deeds and ill deeds.
      Devote yourself to this Yoga: it is the secret of success in work.

51   The steadfast in wisdom, the steadfast of mind,
      giving up the fruits of action, achieve the perfect state.

52   When your mind is no longer obscured by desire,
      repose will come to you concerning what is heard and
          what is yet to be heard.

53   When your mind, so long whirled in conflicting thought,
          achieves poise, and steadies itself in itself,
      you will have realized Yoga.

अर्जुन उवाच

स्थितप्रज्ञस्य का भाषा समाधिस्थस्य केशव ।
स्थितधी: किं प्रभाषेत किमासीत व्रजेत किम् ॥ ५४ ॥

श्रीभगवानुवाच

प्रजहाति यदा कामान्सर्वान्पार्थ मनोगतान् ।
आत्मन्येवात्मना तुष्ट: स्थितप्रज्ञस्तदोच्यते ॥ ५५ ॥

दु:खेष्वनुद्विग्नमना: सुखेषु विगतस्पृह: ।
वीतरागभयक्रोध: स्थितधीर्मुनिरुच्यते ॥ ५६ ॥

य: सर्वत्रानभिस्नेहस्तत्तत्प्राप्य शुभाशुभम् ।
नाभिनन्दति न द्वेष्टि तस्य प्रज्ञा प्रतिष्ठिता ॥ ५७ ॥

यदा संहरते चायं कूर्मोऽङ्गानीव सर्वश: ।
इन्द्रियाणीन्द्रियार्थेभ्यस्तस्य प्रज्ञा प्रतिष्ठिता ॥ ५८ ॥

विषया विनिवर्तन्ते निराहारस्य देहिन: ।
रसवर्जं रसोऽप्यस्य परं दृष्ट्वां निवर्तते ॥ ५९ ॥

यततो ह्यपि कौन्तेय पुरुषस्य विपश्चित: ।
इन्द्रियाणि प्रमाथीनि हरन्ति प्रसभं मन: ॥ ६० ॥

तानि सर्वाणि संयम्य युक्त आसीत मत्पर: ।
वशे हि यस्येन्द्रियाणि तस्य प्रज्ञा प्रतिष्ठिता ॥ ६१ ॥

ध्यायतो विषयान्पुंस: सङ्गस्तेषूपजायते ।
सङ्गात्संजायते काम: कामात्क्रोधोऽभिजायते ॥ ६२ ॥

क्रोधाद्भवति सम्मोह: सम्मोहात्स्मृतिविभ्रम: ।
स्मृतिभ्रंशाद् बुद्धिनाशो बुद्धिनाशात्प्रणश्यति ॥ ६३ ॥

54   Arjuna asked:
       Who is the man of poise, Krishna?
           Who is steady in devotion?
       How does he speak, rest, walk?

55   Krishna answered:
       He has shed desire;
       he is content in the atman by the atman.

56   He is steady. He endures sorrow.
       He does not chase pleasure. Attachment,
           anger and fear do not touch him.

57   He is not selfish. He does not rejoice in prosperity.
       He is not saddened by want.

58   He can recall his senses from their objects
       as the tortoise pulls in its head. He is serene.

59   Objects scatter away from the good but lazy man,
           but desire remains.
       In the perfect state, however, desire also goes.

60   Yes, it is true that the violent senses
       rock the reason of the wisest man.

61   But the steadfast man thinks of me,
           and commands his desires.
       His mind is stable, because his desires are subdued.

62   Meditation on objects breeds attachment;
           from attachment springs covetousness;
       and covetousness breeds anger.

63   Anger leads to confusion,
           and confusion kills discrimination;
       discrimination gone, choice is rendered impossible;
           and when moral choice fails, man is doomed.

रागद्वेषवियुक्तैस्तु विषयानिन्द्रियैश्चरन् ।
आत्मवश्यैर्विधेयात्मा प्रसादमधिगच्छति ॥ ६४ ॥

प्रसादे सर्वदुःखानां हानिरस्योपजायते ।
प्रसन्नचेतसो ह्याशु बुद्धिः पर्यवतिष्ठते ॥ ६५ ॥

नास्ति बुद्धिरयुक्तस्य न चायुक्तस्य भावना ।
न चाभावयतः शान्तिरशान्तस्य कुतः सुखम् ॥ ६६ ॥

इन्द्रियाणां हि चरतां यन्मनोऽनु विधीयते ।
तदस्य हरति प्रज्ञां वायुर्नावमिवाम्भसि ॥ ६७ ॥

तस्माद्यस्य महाबाहो निगृहीतानि सर्वशः ।
इन्द्रियाणीन्द्रियार्थेभ्यस्तस्य प्रज्ञा प्रतिष्ठिता ॥ ६८ ॥

या निशा सर्वभूतानां तस्यां जागर्ति संयमी ।
यस्यां जाग्रति भूतानि सा निशा पश्यतो मुनेः ॥ ६९ ॥

आपूर्यमाणमचलप्रतिष्ठं
　　समुद्रमापः प्रविशन्ति यद्वत् ।
तद्वत्कामा यं प्रविशन्ति सर्वे
　　स शान्तिमाप्नोति न कामकामी ॥ ७० ॥

विहाय कामान्यः सर्वान्पुमांश्चरति निःस्पृहः ।
निर्ममो निरहङ्कारः स शान्तिमधिगच्छति ॥ ७१ ॥

एषा ब्राह्मी स्थितिः पार्थ नैनां प्राप्य विमुह्यति ।
स्थित्वास्यामन्तकालेऽपि ब्रह्मनिर्वाणमृच्छति ॥ ७२ ॥

64   But a person who is established in firmness,
          free from pleasure and repugnance,
      traversing experience with his senses restrained —
          such a person finds tranquillity.

65   When tranquillity comes, sorrow goes;
      a person whose wisdom is tranquil is truly stable.

66   The wavering person does not grow.
      Without growth, there is no peace; without peace, there
          is no bliss.

67   The mind is swayed by the senses;
      they destroy discrimination, as a storm sinks boats on a lake.

68   Only that man can be described as steady
      whose feelings are detached from their objects.

69   What is night to others is daylight to the restrained man;
      and when dawn comes to others, night comes to the
          perceiving sage.

70   The ocean, deep and silent, absorbs a thousand waters.
      The saint absorbs a thousand desires, and finds peace —
          which the satisfier of the senses cannot.

71   Undistracted, passionless, egoless,
      he finds peace.

72   Peace is to be in Brahman, Arjuna, to suffer no more delusion.
      In peace is eternal unity with Brahman, the peace of Nirvana.

THE YOGA OF ACTION

*F*ine, argues Arjuna: the
steady-minded man is superior, because his mind thinks clearly.
If mind, reason, thought, knowledge are so precious, why not stick to
contemplation, which is pure, instead of recommending action, which
is physical, impure? Why say: 'Fight?' Why not just: 'Think?'

Krishna's answer is the key shloka 35 of Canto III: 'shreyam-
svadharma' (one's own dharma is the best). At any given time, a human
being stands at the crossroads of four dharmas: sva-dharma (me-ness;
self-preservation), kula-dharma (family duties; genealogical roots);
yuga-dharma (the spirit of the age, the nexus of the epoch; say, Marxism,
capitalism, Freudianism, feminism in the twentieth century), and
sanatana-dharma (the eternal values that mankind cannot change
but which persuade mankind to change itself into, hopefully, a better,
nobler, more 'human' species).

Arjuna is caught in a conflict of four dharmas. He thinks his sva-
dharma is to lay down arms; his family Kshatriya dharma advises him
to do battle; the dharma of the Dvapara-Yuga demands taking sides in
the doomsday clash; and the sanatana dharma states that all life is
sacred and the atman cannot perish.

Which dharma should he choose? Only the naive, facile and over-
zealous will say that sanatana dharma is always the best. Krishna's
advice seems to be: Remember the hierarchy: lowest is the flesh; then
come the senses; then the mind; the intellect; the atman. Steady yourself
with your Self (samstabhi-atmanam-atmana) —and choose. That is
your dharma — that is the right choice.

अर्जुन उवाच

ज्यायसी चेत्कर्मणस्ते मता बुद्धिर्जनार्दन ।
तत्किं कर्मणि घोरे मां नियोजयसि केशव ॥ १ ॥

व्यामिश्रेणेव वाक्येन बुद्धिं मोहयसीव मे ।
तदेकं वद निश्चित्य येन श्रेयोऽहमाप्नुयाम् ॥ २ ॥

श्रीभगवानुवाच

लोकेऽस्मिन्द्विविधा निष्ठा पुरा प्रोक्ता मयानघ ।
ज्ञानयोगेन सांख्यानां कर्मयोगेन योगिनाम् ॥ ३ ॥

न कर्मणामनारम्भान्नैष्कर्म्यं पुरुषोऽश्नुते ।
न च संन्यसनादेव सिद्धिं समधिगच्छति ॥ ४ ॥

न हि कश्चित्क्षणमपि जातु तिष्ठत्यकर्मकृत् ।
कार्यते ह्यवशः कर्म सर्वः प्रकृतिजैर्गुणैः ॥ ५ ॥

कर्मेन्द्रियाणि संयम्य य आस्ते मनसा स्मरन् ।
इन्द्रियार्थान्विमूढात्मा मिथ्याचारः स उच्यते ॥ ६ ॥

यस्त्विन्द्रियाणि मनसा नियम्यारभतेऽर्जुन ।
कर्मेन्द्रियैः कर्मयोगमसक्तः स विशिष्यते ॥ ७ ॥

नियतं कुरु कर्म त्वं कर्म ज्यायो ह्यकर्मणः ।
शरीरयात्रापि च ते न प्रसिद्ध्येदकर्मणः ॥ ८ ॥

यज्ञार्थात्कर्मणोऽन्यत्र लोकोऽयं कर्मबन्धनः ।
तदर्थं कर्म कौन्तेय मुक्तसङ्गः समाचर ॥ ९ ॥

सहयज्ञाः प्रजाः सृष्ट्वा पुरोवाच प्रजापतिः ।
अनेन प्रसविष्यध्वमेष वोऽस्त्विष्टकामधुक् ॥ १० ॥

देवान्भावयतानेन ते देवा भावयन्तु वः ।
परस्परं भावयन्तः श्रेयः परमवाप्स्यथ ॥ ११ ॥

इष्टान्भोगान्हि वो देवा दास्यन्ते यज्ञभाविताः ।
तैर्दत्तानप्रदायैभ्यो यो भुङ्क्ते स्तेन एव सः ॥ १२ ॥

1   Arjuna asked:
    If, as you say, Krishna, knowledge excels action,
    why do you urge me to this terrible war?

2   You bewilder me with confusing speech:
    tell me that one truth by which I may find you.

3   Krishna replied:
    From the beginning, two methods are offered:
    for the contemplative the Yoga of knowledge,
        for the active the Yoga of action.

4   No one reaches perfection through inaction:
    no one reaches perfection by renouncing work.

5   For look, not a moment gives rest,
        not a moment is without work.
    The senses, products of Nature, compel all to work.

6   He is a fool and a scoundrel who, abstaining from action
    nevertheless sits and dreams up sensual visions.

7   But he excels, who commands his senses by his mind,
    and progresses in the Yoga of work.

8   To work is better than not to work. Inaction will not
        keep even the body together.
    Therefore, Arjuna, work, but work selflessly.

9   All deeds are traps, except disciplined deeds.
    Hence the need for selfless action.

10 When the world was created, Prajapati said:
    'This world will be your wish-fulfilling cow.'

11 Worship the gods with this, and they will listen;
    and mutually shall the great good come.

12 The gods will satisfy your desires. He is a thief,
    who takes satisfaction, and gives back nothing.

यज्ञशिष्टाशिनः सन्तो मुच्यन्ते सर्वकिल्बिषैः ।
भुञ्जते ते त्वघं पापा ये पचन्त्यात्मकारणात् ॥ १३ ॥

अन्नाद्भवन्ति भूतानि पर्जन्यादन्नसंभवः ।
यज्ञाद्भवति पर्जन्यो यज्ञः कर्मसमुद्भवः ॥ १४ ॥

कर्म ब्रह्मोद्भवं विद्धि ब्रह्माक्षरसमुद्भवम् ।
तस्मात्सर्वगतं ब्रह्म नित्यं यज्ञे प्रतिष्ठितम् ॥ १५ ॥

एवं प्रवर्तितं चक्रं नानुवर्तयतीह यः ।
अघायुरिन्द्रियारामो मोघं पार्थ स जीवति ॥१६॥

यस्त्वात्मरतिरेव स्यादात्मतृप्तश्च मानवः ।
आत्मन्येव च संतुष्टस्तस्य कार्यं न विद्यते ॥ १७ ॥

नैव तस्य कृतेनार्थो नाकृतेनेह कश्चन ।
न चास्य सर्वभूतेषु कश्चिदर्थव्यपाश्रयः ॥ १८ ॥

तस्मादसक्तः सततं कार्यं कर्म समाचर ।
असक्तो ह्याचरन्कर्म परमाप्नोति पूरुषः ॥ १९ ॥

कर्मणैव हि संसिद्धिमास्थिता जनकादयः ।
लोकसंग्रहमेवापि संपश्यन्कर्तुमर्हसि ॥ २० ॥

यद्यदाचरति श्रेष्ठस्तत्तदेवेतरो जनः ।
स यत्प्रमाणं कुरुते लोकस्तदनुवर्तते ॥ २१ ॥

न मे पार्थास्ति कर्तव्यं त्रिषु लोकेषु किंचन ।
नानवाप्तमवाप्तव्यं वर्त एव च कर्मणि ॥ २२ ॥

यदि ह्यहं न वर्तेयं जातु कर्मण्यतन्द्रितः ।
मम वर्त्मानुवर्तन्ते मनुष्याः पार्थ सर्वशः ॥ २३ ॥

उत्सीदेयुरिमे लोका न कुर्यां कर्म चेदहम् ।
संकरस्य च कर्ता स्यामुपहन्यामिमाः प्रजाः ॥ २४ ॥

सक्ताः कर्मण्यविद्वांसो यथा कुर्वन्ति भारत ।
कुर्याद्विद्वांस्तथासक्तश्चिकीर्षुर्लोकसंग्रहम् ॥ २५ ॥

13 Those who eat sanctified food, are cleansed of wrong,
    but the selfish who eat for themselves, eat filth.

14 Food is the cause of life, from rain is food born;
    ritual produces rain, and ritual is born of karma.

15 Karma comes from the Vedas, and the Vedas from Brahma.
    Brahma depends on worship.

16 His life is futile, who is not aware of this wheel's revolutions,
    who lives merely to wallow in his senses.

17 But he who is merged in the atman, content in the atman,
        at peace in the atman,
    for him deeds are not fetters.

18 To work and not to work mean nothing to him;
    he does not need outside help.

19 Do what must be done, Arjuna, and do it selflessly;
    selfless action is the path to perfection.

20 Through work did Janaka and others reach perfection;
    do your work for the good of your fellow-beings.

21 People will always imitate a superior,
    following the example set by his action.

22 I have no duty, I have nothing not attained and nothing
        to attain,
    yet even I persist in work.

23 For if I were to stop working,
    men would follow my example.

24 If I did not work, the three worlds would crumble,
    judgment would blur, chaos follow, and all beings perish.

25 The wise man must act, even as the work-obsessed fool does,
    but shedding selfishness, and pursuing knowledge.

न बुद्धिभेदं जनयेदज्ञानां कर्मसङ्गिनाम् ।
जोषयेत्सर्वकर्माणि विद्वान्युक्तः समाचरन् ॥ २६ ॥

प्रकृतेः क्रियमाणानि गुणैः कर्माणि सर्वशः ।
अहङ्कारविमूढात्मा कर्ताहमिति मन्यते ॥ २७ ॥

तत्त्ववित्तु महाबाहो गुणकर्मविभागयोः ।
गुणा गुणेषु वर्तन्त इति मत्वा न सज्जते ॥ २८ ॥

प्रकृतेर्गुणसंमूढाः सज्जन्ते गुणकर्मसु ।
तानकृत्स्नविदो मन्दान्कृत्स्नविन्न विचालयेत् ॥ २९ ॥

मयि सर्वाणि कर्माणि संन्यस्याध्यात्मचेतसा ।
निराशीर्निर्ममो भूत्वा युध्यस्व विगतज्वरः ॥ ३० ॥

ये मे मतमिदं नित्यमनुतिष्ठन्ति मानवाः ।
श्रद्धावन्तोऽनसूयन्तो मुच्यन्ते तेऽपि कर्मभिः ॥ ३१ ॥

ये त्वेतदभ्यसूयन्तो नानुतिष्ठन्ति मे मतम् ।
सर्वज्ञानविमूढांस्तान्विद्धि नष्टानचेतसः ॥ ३२ ॥

सदृशं चेष्टते स्वस्याः प्रकृतेर्ज्ञानवानपि ।
प्रकृतिं यान्ति भूतानि निग्रहः किं करिष्यति ॥ ३३ ॥

इन्द्रियस्येन्द्रियस्यार्थे रागद्वेषौ व्यवस्थितौ ।
तयोर्न वशमागच्छेत्तौ ह्यस्य परिपन्थिनौ ॥ ३४ ॥

श्रेयान्स्वधर्मो विगुणः परधर्मात्स्वनुष्ठितात् ।
स्वधर्मे निधनं श्रेयः परधर्मो भयावहः ॥ ३५ ॥

अर्जुन उवाच
अथ केन प्रयुक्तोऽयं पापं चरति पूरुषः ।
अनिच्छन्नपि वार्ष्णेय बलादिव नियोजितः ॥ ३६ ॥

26   Leave aside the fool's work-centred reasoning;
      let the learned learn more through selfless work.

27   All action is performed by the senses;
      confused by his ego, man thinks 'I am the doer'.

28   But the man who sees the nature of matter and the
          nature of karma,
      who sees how the senses play on the senses, he is not deceived.

29   There is no need for those who know truth to humiliate
          the dull-witted workers who are attached to the senses,
      and deceived by the senses.

30   Offer all your actions to Me, and take rest in the atman,
      crush hope and the ego, and fight —rid of your doubts.

31   They also escape the fetters of action
      who devote themselves to Me, in full faith.

32   But those who carp, and shun my teaching,
      and, confusing themselves, lose clear vision, they are doomed.

33   Even the wisest man must conform to his nature.
      How will stubbornness help?

34   Desire and disgust are products of nature.
      No man should live in the shadow of either —
          they are his deadly enemies.

35   One's own dharma, however imperfect, is better than
          another's, however perfect.
      Better death in one's own dharma; another's dharma can
          be treacherous.

36   Arjuna asked:
      But what is it, Krishna,
      that propels man to wrong-doing against his true desire?

श्री भगवानुवाच

काम एष क्रोध एष रजोगुणसमुद्भवः ।
महाशनो महापाप्मा विद्ध्येनमिह वैरिणम् ॥ ३७ ॥

धूमेनाव्रियते वह्निर्यथादर्शो मलेन च ।
यथोल्बेनावृतो गर्भस्तथा तेनेदमावृतम् ॥ ३८ ॥

आवृतं ज्ञानमेतेन ज्ञानिनो नित्यवैरिणा ।
कामरूपेण कौन्तेय दुष्पूरेणानलेन च ॥ ३९ ॥

इन्द्रियाणि मनो बुद्धिरस्याधिष्ठानमुच्यते ।
एतैर्विमोहयत्येष ज्ञानमावृत्य देहिनम् ॥ ४० ॥

तस्मात्त्वमिन्द्रियाण्यादौ नियम्य भरतर्षभ ।
पाप्मानं प्रजहि ह्येनं ज्ञानविज्ञाननाशनम् ॥ ४१ ॥

इन्द्रियाणि पराण्याहुरिन्द्रियेभ्यः परं मनः ।
मनसस्तु परा बुद्धिर्यो बुद्धेः परतस्तु सः ॥ ४२ ॥

एवं बुद्धेः परं बुद्ध्वा संस्तभ्यात्मानमात्मना ।
जहि शत्रुं महाबाहो कामरूपं दुरासदम् ॥ ४३ ॥

37   Krishna replied:
     It is greed, Arjuna, and it is anger, created by the terrible
         and heinous rajas-guna.
     Treat them as your enemies.

38   As smoke smothers fire, as dust films glass,
     as womb enfolds seed, so greed destroys judgment.

39   Greed is a fierce fire.
     It destroys judgment. It fools the wise.

40   It hides in the mind, the intellect and the senses.
     It destroys the atman by working through them.

41   Therefore, first control the senses.
     Destroy this heinous enemy of knowledge.

42   They say the senses are higher than the flesh;
         the mind is higher than the senses;
     the intellect is higher than the mind,
         and the atman higher that the intellect.

43   Steady the atman in the atman.
     Strengthened by pure consciousness,
         destroy the great enemy called kama!

THE YOGA OF ACTION AND RENUNCIATION

*S*ince there are four dharmas simultaneously operating and no guarantee that people will make the right choice, ups and downs in the course of over-all Dharma are inevitable. However, the cosmos is fitted with a self-correcting mechanism. This 'mechanism' is explained in the key shloka 7 of Canto IV, a shloka· that most Hindus know by heart and are prone to repeat whenever they feel that things are falling apart, as if it were some kind of magic panacea: 'When Dharma declines, and adharma flourishes, I give myself birth, to restore the balance.' Divinity is not born; only creatures caught in the coils of karma get born and re-born. Divinity gives itself birth as and when required. The implication is that, just as there is Krishna present to console, advise and inspire Arjuna, his devotee (bhakta) and friend (sakha), so there is always a divine presence for anyone ready to receive spiritual guidance. Knock — and the door opens.

The important thing is to realize that all action must be treated as 'ritual' (yajna) not as sensual. In ritual action, selflessness, dedication and sacrifice are of the essence. All action is service, but not to oneself. The concept of service purifies action of selfishness. This liberates the doer from the hell brought by ill karma, and equally from the heaven of good karma. Both hell and heaven are seen in Hinduism as temporary after-life punishments for ill deeds and good deeds. The secret is to see inaction in action ('ritual' unself-conscious action brings no fruits, good or bad); and action in inaction ('selfish' knowledge brings fruits, good or bad).

श्रीभगवानुवाच

इमं विवस्वते योगं प्रोक्तवानहमव्ययम् ।
विवस्वान्मनवे प्राह मनुरिक्ष्वाकवेऽब्रवीत् ॥ १ ॥

एवं परम्पराप्राप्तमिमं राजर्षयो विदुः ।
स कालेनेह महता योगो नष्टः परंतप ॥ २ ॥

स एवायं मया तेऽद्य योगः प्रोक्तः पुरातनः ।
भक्तोऽसि मे सखा चेति रहस्यं ह्येतदुत्तमम् ॥ ३ ॥

अर्जुन उवाच

अपरं भवतो जन्म परं जन्म विवस्वतः ।
कथमेतद्विजानीयां त्वमादौ प्रोक्तवानिति ॥ ४ ॥

श्रीभगवानुवाच

बहूनि मे व्यतीतानि जन्मानि तव चार्जुन ।
तान्यहं वेद सर्वाणि न त्वं वेत्थ परंतप ॥ ५ ॥

अजोऽपि सन्नव्ययात्मा भूतानामीश्वरोऽपि सन् ।
प्रकृतिं स्वामधिष्ठाय संभवाम्यात्ममायया ॥ ६ ॥

यदा यदा हि धर्मस्य ग्लानिर्भवति भारत ।
अभ्युत्थानमधर्मस्य तदात्मानं सृजाम्यहम् ॥ ७ ॥

परित्राणाय साधूनां विनाशाय च दुष्कृताम् ।
धर्मसंस्थापनार्थाय संभवामि युगे युगे ॥ ८ ॥

जन्म कर्म च मे दिव्यमेवं यो वेत्ति तत्त्वतः ।
त्यक्त्वा देहं पुनर्जन्म नैति मामेति सोऽर्जुन ॥ ९ ॥

वीतरागभयक्रोधा मन्मया मामुपाश्रिताः ।
बहवो ज्ञानतपसा पूता मद्भावमागताः ॥ १० ॥

1   Krishna continued:
     To Vivasvat I gave this eternal discipline;
     Vivasvat told it to Manu, Manu to Ikshvaku.

2   So its continuity was assured,
         and the royal saints understood it;
     but as time passed, its significance declined.

3   Today, because you respect me,
         and because you are my friend,
     I give you this timeless, mysterious, and profound discipline.

4   Arjuna asked:
     But you were born later than Vivasvat;
     and yet you say you gave it to him. What do you mean?

5   Krishna replied:
     You, and I, have seen many births —
     I can recall them all, but you cannot.

6   I am birthless, and changeless, I am the Lord.
     I am born through the power of my maya.

7   When dharma declines, and adharma flourishes,
     I give myself birth, to restore the balance.

8   And every age witnesses my birth;
         I come to protect the good, and destroy the wicked.
     I come to re-establish dharma,

9   The man who approves the divinity of my birth
         and the miracle of my work,
     discards his body, and is not born again.

10   Free from greed, fear and anger, merged in me,
         sheltering in me,
     purified by the discipline of knowledge, many have
         known me.

ये यथा मां प्रपद्यन्ते तांस्तथैव भजाम्यहम् ।
मम वर्त्मानुवर्तन्ते मनुष्याः पार्थ सर्वशः ॥ ११ ॥

काङ्क्षन्तः कर्मणां सिद्धिं यजन्त इह देवताः ।
क्षिप्रं हि मानुषे लोके सिद्धिर्भवति कर्मजा ॥ १२ ॥

चातुर्वर्ण्यं मया सृष्टं गुणकर्मविभागशः ।
तस्य कर्तारमपि मां विद्ध्यकर्तारमव्ययम् ॥ १३ ॥

न मां कर्माणि लिम्पन्ति न मे कर्मफले स्पृहा ।
इति मां योऽभिजानाति कर्मभिर्न स बध्यते ॥ १४ ॥

एवं ज्ञात्वा कृतं कर्म पूर्वैरपि मुमुक्षुभिः ।
कुरु कर्मैव तस्मात्त्वं पूर्वैः पूर्वतरं कृतम् ॥ १५ ॥

किं कर्म किमकर्मेति कवयोऽप्यत्र मोहिताः ।
तत्ते कर्म प्रवक्ष्यामि यज्ज्ञात्वा मोक्ष्यसेऽशुभात् ॥ १६ ॥

कर्मणो ह्यपि बोद्धव्यं बोद्धव्यं च विकर्मणः ।
अकर्मणश्च बोद्धव्यं गहना कर्मणो गतिः ॥ १७ ॥

कर्मण्यकर्म यः पश्येदकर्मणि च कर्म यः ।
स बुद्धिमान्मनुष्येषु स युक्तः कृत्स्नकर्मकृत् ॥ १८ ॥

यस्य सर्वे समारम्भाः कामसंकल्पवर्जिताः ।
ज्ञानाग्निदग्धकर्माणं तमाहुः पण्डितं बुधाः ॥ १९ ॥

त्यक्त्वा कर्मफलासङ्गं नित्यतृप्तो निराश्रयः ।
कर्मण्यभिप्रवृत्तोऽपि नैव किञ्चित्करोति सः ॥ २० ॥

निराशीर्यतचित्तात्मा त्यक्तसर्वपरिग्रहः ।
शारीरं केवलं कर्म कुर्वन्नाप्नोति किल्बिषम् ॥ २१ ॥

11   I satisfy all, whatever the form of worship.
      My path is the path all follow, in different ways.

12   Men worship gods in the hope of material gain —
      they know work brings quick results.

13   Though I am the creator of the four castes on the basis
          of guna and karma,
      I am not really their creator.

14   For I have no desire for the fruits of action.
      So work does not fetter me. To know this is to be free.

15   Sages in the past, seeking perfection, knew this,
          and knowing it, progressed.
      Learn from their example.

16   What is work? and what is not work? are questions that
          perplex the wisest of men.
      Let me instruct you on the nature of work, and remove
          your confusion.

17   Karma is a great mystery, but what is work one must know,
      and what is not work, and what prohibited work.

18   That man knows what work is,
          who sees action in inaction, and inaction in action.
      He is wise.

19   And if he works selflessly, if his actions are purified
      in the fire of knowledge, he will be called wise by the learned.

20   He abandons greed; he is content; he is self-sufficient;
      he works, yet such a man cannot be said to work.

21   If he forsakes hope, restrains his mind, and relinquishes
          reward —
      he works, yet he does not work.

यदृच्छालाभसंतुष्टो द्वन्द्वातीतो विमत्सरः ।
समः सिद्धावसिद्धौ च कृत्वापि न निबध्यते ॥ २२ ॥

गतसङ्गस्य मुक्तस्य ज्ञानावस्थितचेतसः ।
यज्ञायाचरतः कर्म समग्रं प्रविलीयते ॥ २३ ॥

ब्रह्मार्पणं ब्रह्म हविर्ब्रह्माग्नौ ब्रह्मणा हुतम् ।
ब्रह्मैव तेन गन्तव्यं ब्रह्मकर्मसमाधिना ॥ २४ ॥

दैवमेवापरे यज्ञं योगिनः पर्युपासते ।
ब्रह्माग्रावपरे यज्ञं यज्ञेनैवोपजुह्वति ॥ २५ ॥

श्रोत्रादीनीन्द्रियाण्यन्ये संयमाग्निषु जुह्वति ।
शब्दादीन्विषयानन्य इन्द्रियाग्निषु जुह्वति ॥ २६ ॥

सर्वाणीन्द्रियकर्माणि प्राणकर्माणि चापरे ।
आत्मसंयमयोगाग्नौ जुह्वति ज्ञानदीपिते ॥ २७ ॥

द्रव्ययज्ञास्तपोयज्ञा योगयज्ञास्तथापरे ।
स्वाध्यायज्ञानयज्ञाश्च यतयः संशितव्रताः ॥ २८ ॥

अपाने जुह्वति प्राणं प्राणेऽपानं तथापरे ।
प्राणापानगती रुद्ध्वा प्राणायामपरायणाः ॥ २९ ॥

अपरे नियताहाराः प्राणान्प्राणेषु जुह्वति ।
सर्वेऽप्येते यज्ञविदो यज्ञक्षपितकल्मषाः ॥ ३० ॥

यज्ञशिष्टामृतभुजो यान्ति ब्रह्म सनातनम् ।
नायं लोकोऽस्त्ययज्ञस्य कुतोऽन्यः कुरुसत्तम ॥ ३१ ॥

एवं बहुविधा यज्ञा वितता ब्रह्मणो मुखे ।
कर्मजान्विद्धि तान्सर्वानेवं ज्ञात्वा विमोक्ष्यसे ॥ ३२ ॥

22   He is satisfied with whatever comes, unaffected by extremes,
          free from jealousy,
      he maintains poise in failure and success —
          his deeds do not fetter him.

23   His karma disappears, his work is all discipline;
      he is free from greed, he is steady in knowledge.

24   'The ritual is Brahman, the offering is Brahman,
          given by Brahman in the fire of Brahman' —
      such absorption in Brahman takes him to Brahman.

25   Some yogis sacrifice to the gods,
      others pay homage by offering the atman in the fire of
          Brahman.

26   Some offer their senses as homage,
      others offer the objects of the senses.

27   Some offer the work of the body and the vital breath of life,
      in the fire of self-control, lit by knowledge.

28   Some offer wealth, others penance, and still others Yoga;
      some, controlled and dedicated, offer wisdom and learning.

29   Some channelise their vital life-breaths, the prana and apana.
      They concentrate on breath-restraint.

30   Still others, digesting food, offer the body's functions.
      They have realized the meaning of discipline and are
          purified by it.

31   They eat the fruits of discipline,
          and reach the eternal Brahman.
      Even this world is not for the man without discipline;
          how will he gain a better one, Arjuna?

32   Discipline shows the face of Brahma.
      It is the product of action. Know this, and be free.

श्रेयान्द्रव्यमयाद्यज्ञाज्ज्ञानयज्ञः परंतप ।
सर्वं कर्माखिलं पार्थ ज्ञाने परिसमाप्यते ॥ ३३ ॥

तद्विद्धि प्रणिपातेन परिप्रश्नेन सेवया ।
उपदेक्ष्यन्ति ते ज्ञानं ज्ञानिनस्तत्त्वदर्शिनः ॥ ३४ ॥

यज्ज्ञात्वा न पुनर्मोहमेवं यास्यसि पाण्डव ।
येन भूतान्यशेषेण द्रक्ष्यस्यात्मन्यथो मयि ॥ ३५ ॥

अपि चेदसि पापेभ्यः सर्वेभ्यः पापकृत्तमः ।
सर्वं ज्ञानप्लवेनैव वृजिनं संतरिष्यसि ॥ ३६ ॥

यथैधांसि समिद्धोऽग्निर्भस्मसात्कुरुतेऽर्जुन ।
ज्ञानाग्निः सर्वकर्माणि भस्मसात्कुरुते तथा ॥ ३७ ॥

न हि ज्ञानेन सदृशं पवित्रमिह विद्यते ।
तत्स्वयं योगसंसिद्धः कालेनात्मनि विन्दति ॥ ३८ ॥

श्रद्धावाँल्लभते ज्ञानं तत्परः संयतेन्द्रियः ।
ज्ञानं लब्ध्वा परां शान्तिमचिरेणाधिगच्छति ॥ ३९ ॥

अज्ञश्चाश्रद्दधानश्च संशयात्मा विनश्यति ।
नायं लोकोऽस्ति न परो न सुखं संशयात्मनः ॥ ४० ॥

योगसंन्यस्तकर्माणं ज्ञानसंछिन्नसंशयम् ।
आत्मवन्तं न कर्माणि निबध्नन्ति धनञ्जय ॥ ४१ ॥

तस्मादज्ञानसंभूतं हृत्स्थं ज्ञानासिनात्मनः ।
छित्त्वैनं संशयं योगमातिष्ठोत्तिष्ठ भारत ॥ ४२ ॥

33 Sacrifice of knowledge is superior to sacrifice of wealth;
    action's consummation is wisdom.

34 Be humble, serve others; ask questions, and you shall know;
    the wise who have reached truth, shall instruct you.

35 Knowledge will remove your bewilderment,
    and you will see all creation in yourself and in me.

36 The raft of knowledge ferries
    even the worst ill-doer to safety.

37 As a flaming fire consumes logs into ashes,
    so knowledge consumes karma.

38 There is no purifier like knowledge in this world:
    time makes man see the truth of this.

39 The devoted man, indefatigable commander of his senses,
        gains knowledge;
    with this knowledge he finds the final peace.

40 The ignorant, the disrespectful, the disbelieving, await ruin.
    The doubt-ridden find joy neither in this world
        nor in the next.

41 Work will not fetter him who shelters in the atman.
    Discipline purifies his work, Arjuna, and knowledge
        dissipates his disbelief.

42 Slice with the sword of knowledge this disbelief in the atman!
    Disbelief is the product of ignorance.
        Find strength in discipline, and rise, Arjuna!

THE YOGA OF RENUNCIATION

*T*o Arjuna, wondering why *renunciation of work (which is what he thinks he is doing by refusing to fight) is treated by Krishna on a par with performance of work (which Arjuna considers as inferior), Krishna gives a categorical answer in the key second shloka of Canto X: 'Renunciation and activity both liberate, but to work is better than to renounce.'*

No question of it — the Gita *is the gospel of action, selfless action, fruit-forsaking action.*

Gracefully, almost unobtrusively, Krishna brings in here the Upanishadic concepts of the Witness and the Participant. Two birds sit on the golden bough of the pippala tree, says the Shvetashvatara Upanishad. One bird eats the sweet fruit, the other watches the first bird eat. Both are happy. One is happier. Which? And why?

Our body is the sweet, sensual pippala tree. The atman is the watching bird. Our deeds are the eating bird. The watching stops when the tree withers and dies, and the watching bird flies away. Till that time, eating and watching proceed simultaneously. So the advice of Krishna is simple. Watch life detachedly. Enjoy it coolly. Savour your deeds as you would the performance of an actor in a play. Be involved — and yet be free. As he says in shlokas 8 and 9: 'Seeing, listening, eating, talking, breathing...he should say, "I do nothing at all, only my senses are busy." '

अर्जुन उवाच

संन्यासं कर्मणां कृष्ण पुनर्योगं च शंससि ।
यच्छ्रेय एतयोरेकं तन्मे ब्रूहि सुनिश्चितम् ॥ १ ॥

श्रीभगवानुवाच

संन्यासः कर्मयोगश्च निःश्रेयसकरावुभौ ।
तयोस्तु कर्मसंन्यासात्कर्मयोगो विशिष्यते ॥ २ ॥

ज्ञेयः स नित्यसंन्यासी यो न द्वेष्टि न काङ्क्षति ।
निर्द्वन्द्वो हि महाबाहो सुखं बन्धात्प्रमुच्यते ॥ ३ ॥

सांख्ययोगौ पृथग्बालाः प्रवदन्ति न पण्डिताः ।
एकमप्यास्थितः सम्यगुभयोर्विन्दते फलम् ॥ ४ ॥

यत्सांख्यैः प्राप्यते स्थानं तद्योगैरपि गम्यते ।
एकं सांख्यं च योगं च यः पश्यति स पश्यति ॥ ५ ॥

संन्यासस्तु महाबाहो दुःखमातुमयोगतः ।
योगयुक्तो मुनिर्ब्रह्म नचिरेणाधिगच्छति ॥ ६ ॥

योगयुक्तो विशुद्धात्मा विजितात्मा जितेन्द्रियः ।
सर्वभूतात्मभूतात्मा कुर्वन्नपि न लिप्यते ॥ ७ ॥

नैव किंचित्करोमीति युक्तो मन्येत तत्त्ववित् ।
पश्यञ्शृण्वन्स्पृशञ्जिघ्रन्नश्नन्गच्छन्स्वपञ्श्वसन् ॥ ८ ॥

प्रलपन्विसृजन्गृह्णन्नुन्मिषन्निमिषन्नपि ।
इन्द्रियाणीन्द्रियार्थेषु वर्तन्त इति धारयन् ॥ ९ ॥

ब्रह्मण्याधाय कर्माणि सङ्गं त्यक्त्वा करोति यः ।
लिप्यते न स पापेन पद्मपत्रमिवाम्भसा ॥ १० ॥

कायेन मनसा बुद्ध्या केवलैरिन्द्रियैरपि ।
योगिनः कर्म कुर्वन्ति सङ्गं त्यक्त्वात्मशुद्धये ॥ ११ ॥

1   Arjuna asked:
     First you say 'Renounce', Krishna, then you say, 'Work',
     Which is better? —Tell me clearly.

2   Krishna replied:
     Renunciation and activity both liberate,
     but to work is better than to renounce.

3   He is the constant sannyasi, who neither hates nor desires;
     free from extremes, his salvation progresses.

4   The ignorant, not the learned, think the two are different.
     If one is practised in earnest, the rewards of both are received.

5   The strivers in work reach the fulfilment of the strivers in
          renunciation.
     See both as the same, and you see the truth.

6   Renunciation is very difficult, Arjuna;
     but the sage, spurred to work by wisdom,
          soon finds Brahman.

7   A man who commands his senses and vanquishes his body,
          who sees one's atman as the Atman in all,
     who purifies his mind before he performs his deeds —such
          a man is not sullied.

8   Though seeing, listening, smelling, eating, walking,
     sleeping, breathing, talking, holding, and discarding,

9   He should say,
     'I do nothing at all, only my senses are busy.'

10   As a lotus leaf will not be stained by slime,
     so the detached person, offering his deeds to Brahman,
          will not be stained by work.

11   Yogis work with the body, the mind and the senses,
     but abandon greed, in order to purify the atman.

युक्तः कर्मफलं त्यक्त्वा शान्तिमाप्नोति नैष्ठिकीम् ।
अयुक्तः कामकारेण फले सक्तो निबध्यते ॥ १२ ॥

सर्वकर्माणि मनसा संन्यस्यास्ते सुखं वशी ।
नवद्वारे पुरे देही नैव कुर्वन्न कारयन् ॥ १३ ॥

न कर्तृत्वं न कर्माणि लोकस्य सृजति प्रभुः ।
न कर्मफलसंयोगं स्वभावस्तु प्रवर्तते ॥ १४ ॥

नादत्ते कस्यचित्पापं न चैव सुकृतं विभुः ।
अज्ञानेनावृतं ज्ञानं तेन मुह्यन्ति जन्तवः ॥ १५ ॥

ज्ञानेन तु तदज्ञानं येषां नाशितमात्मनः ।
तेषामादित्यवज्ज्ञानं प्रकाशयति तत्परम् ॥ १६ ॥

तद्बुद्धयस्तदात्मानस्तन्निष्ठास्तत्परायणाः ।
गच्छन्त्यपुनरावृत्तिं ज्ञाननिर्धूतकल्मषाः ॥ १७ ॥

विद्याविनयसंपन्ने ब्राह्मणे गवि हस्तिनि ।
शुनि चैव श्वपाके च पण्डिताः समदर्शिनः ॥ १८ ॥

इहैव तैर्जितः सर्गो येषां साम्ये स्थितं मनः ।
निर्दोषं हि समं ब्रह्म तस्माद्ब्रह्मणि ते स्थिताः ॥ १९ ॥

न प्रहृष्येत्प्रियं प्राप्य नोद्विजेत्प्राप्य चाप्रियम् ।
स्थिरबुद्धिरसंमूढो ब्रह्मविद् ब्रह्मणि स्थितः ॥ २० ॥

बाह्यस्पर्शेष्वसक्तात्मा विन्दत्यात्मनि यत्सुखम् ।
स ब्रह्मयोगयुक्तात्मा सुखमक्षयमश्नुते ॥ २१ ॥

ये हि संस्पर्शजा भोगा दुःखयोनय एव ते ।
आद्यन्तवन्तः कौन्तेय न तेषु रमते बुधः ॥ २२ ॥

12   Abandoning the fruits of work, the balanced mind attains
         peace;
      but the unsteady mind, motivated by greed, is trapped in
         its own reward.

13   The stable person, renouncing work through knowledge,
         neither acts himself,
      nor forces action on others, but takes refuge in the body,
         the city of the nine gates.

14   Brahman is concerned with neither the doer nor the deed,
      nor the reward of the deed.

15   Brahman does not cause anyone's reward or punishment.
      Wisdom is blocked by ignorance, and delusion is the result.

16   But, like the sun, knowledge reveals Brahman
      to those whose ignorance is removed by self-realization.

17   Washed in the light of knowledge,and never born again,
      are those whose minds are engrossed in the atman,
         whose fulfilment is in the atman.

18   A Brahmin, a cow, a dog, an elephant,
      are all the same to an atman-knower.

19   He has transcended life, he reposes in Brahman,
      his mind is not nervous and agitated.

20   Reposing in Brahman, and maintaining serenity, undeluded,
      the knower of Brahman is not happy with what is pleasant,
         nor unhappy with what is unpleasant.

21   Unaffected by the world, he enjoys the bliss of the atman.
      He achieves eternal peace, sunk in the meditation of Brahman.

22   Restlessness is the product of sensual joys, joys that are
         impermanent, joys that begin and end.
      The wise do not seek pleasure in them.

शक्नोतीहैव यः सोढुं प्राक्शरीरविमोक्षणात् ।
कामक्रोधोद्भवं वेगं स युक्तः स सुखी नरः ॥ २३ ॥

योऽन्तःसुखोऽन्तरारामस्तथान्तर्ज्योतिरेव यः ।
स योगी ब्रह्मनिर्वाणं ब्रह्मभूतोऽधिगच्छति ॥ २४ ॥

लभन्ते ब्रह्मनिर्वाणमृषयः क्षीणकल्मषाः ।
छिन्नद्वैधा यतात्मानः सर्वभूतहिते रताः ॥ २५ ॥

कामक्रोधवियुक्तानां यतीनां यतचेतसाम् ।
अभितो ब्रह्मनिर्वाणं वर्तते विदितात्मनाम् ॥ २६ ॥

स्पर्शान्कृत्वा बहिर्बाह्यांश्चक्षुश्चैवान्तरे भ्रुवोः ।
प्राणापानौ समौ कृत्वा नासाभ्यन्तरचारिणौ ॥ २७ ॥

यतेन्द्रियमनोबुद्धिर्मुनिर्मोक्षपरायणः ।
विगतेच्छाभयक्रोधो यः सदा मुक्त एव सः ॥ २८ ॥

भोक्तारं यज्ञतपसां सर्वलोकमहेश्वरम् ।
सुहृदं सर्वभूतानां ज्ञात्वा मां शान्तिमृच्छति ॥ २९ ॥

23 He is reposed, he is happy,
    who has no anger, who has no desire.

24 Whose contentment lies within, whose repose is within,
        whose glory is within,
    that yogi finds Brahman, and is liberated.

25 All evils discarded, all doubts erased,
    all senses restrained, devoted to service, he is liberated.

26 There is the Nirvana of Brahman for all who strive thus,
    their passions controlled, and their atman realized.

27 Controlling his vision, curbing his life-breaths,
    regulating prana and apana,

28 Commanding his senses, mind and intellect,
    rid of lust, anger and greed, he finds moksha.

29 For he knows me as the giver of ritual and religious
        discipline, the Creator of the worlds,
    and the refuge of all beings; and he finds peace.

THE YOGA OF MEDITATION

*T*he steady-minded person (*sthita-prajna*) who is able to say, truthfully, 'I do nothing at all, only my senses are busy', must be a very rare phenomenon. To dispel Arjuna's fear that he is not the candidate for such high-class spiritual achievement, Krishna provides the key shloka 40 of Canto VI. What matters in Yoga, he says, is not success but sincere effort. 'The struggle for virtue (*kalyana*) is never wasted.'

Peace of mind is not a goal but a process. Krishna goes into some detail on the nature of this process, especially the signs by which it can be recognized. To begin with, the aspirant must discipline desire; he must learn to respect his atman by using it to control his animal impulses; he must discover the pleasures of solitude and solitariness; he must perform daily whatever physical yoga is required to discipline his body; he must practise the principle of the golden mean in every activity; he must look on delight and suffering everywhere as his own.

Such effort and empathy characterize the true Yogi, who is superior to the penance-doers, the learned in theoretical knowledge, and the busily active. Such a person, explains Krishna, may not attain the supreme bliss (*sukhamuttamam*), but 'he is never far from me, and I am never far from him'.

The supreme bliss is not a product of determined seeking after it, but a possible by-product of honest yogic effort to improve the quality of one's humanity.

श्रीभगवानुवाच

अनाश्रितः कर्मफलं कार्यं कर्म करोति यः ।
स संन्यासी च योगी च न निरग्निर्न चाक्रियः ॥ १ ॥

यं संन्यासमिति प्राहुर्योगं तं विद्धि पाण्डव ।
न ह्यसंन्यस्तसंकल्पो योगी भवति कश्चन ॥ २ ॥

आरुरुक्षोर्मुनेर्योगं कर्म कारणमुच्यते ।
योगारूढस्य तस्यैव शमः कारणमुच्यते ॥ ३ ॥

यदा हि नेन्द्रियार्थेषु न कर्मस्वनुषज्जते ।
सर्वसंकल्पसंन्यासी योगारूढस्तदोच्यते ॥ ४ ॥

उद्धरेदात्मनात्मानं नात्मानमवसादयेत् ।
आत्मैव ह्यात्मनो बन्धुरात्मैव रिपुरात्मनः ॥ ५ ॥

बन्धुरात्मात्मनस्तस्य येनात्मैवात्मना जितः ।
अनात्मनस्तु शत्रुत्वे वर्तेतात्मैव शत्रुवत् ॥ ६ ॥

जितात्मनः प्रशान्तस्य परमात्मा समाहितः ।
शीतोष्णसुखदुःखेषु तथा मानापमानयोः ॥ ७ ॥

ज्ञानविज्ञानतृप्तात्मा कूटस्थो विजितेन्द्रियः ।
युक्त इत्युच्यते योगी समलोष्टाश्मकाञ्चनः ॥ ८ ॥

सुहृन्मित्रार्युदासीनमध्यस्थद्वेष्यबन्धुषु ।
साधुष्वपि च पापेषु समबुद्धिर्विशिष्यते ॥ ९ ॥

योगी युञ्जीत सततमात्मानं रहसि स्थितः ।
एकाकी यतचित्तात्मा निराशीरपरिग्रहः ॥ १० ॥

शुचौ देशे प्रतिष्ठाप्य स्थिरमासनमात्मनः ।
नात्युच्छ्रितं नातिनीचं चैलाजिनकुशोत्तरम् ॥ ११ ॥

1   Krishna continued:
     Whoever does his work selflessly combines renunciation
          and activity —
     not one who does not work, or rejects the prescribed duties.

2   Right action is really renunciation.
     No yogi succeeds without discarding desire.

3   The man desirous of Yoga seeks action as the path;
     when Yoga is achieved, serenity takes over.

4   Then he is not bound either to sense-objects or to work,
     then he is rid of all desires.

5   The atman is the means of spiritual achievement.
          On no account should the atman be harmed.
     It is your best friend, do not make it your worst enemy.

6   It is a friend of the man who uses it to subdue it:
     it is an enemy of the man who does not.

7   The atman is the consummation of the tranquil-minded
          and the self-subdued,
     who are serene in heat and cold, disgust and delight,
          honour and infamy.

8   When a clod of earth, stone, and gold become alike,
     serenity is achieved.

9   Serenity is achieved by a man who considers impartially
          his friends, his lovers,
     enemies, judges, kinsmen, even the wicked.

10   Living in solitude, mind and body's passions in check,
     a yogi should strive for absorption in the atman.

11   And he should seat himself in a clean spot, not too high
          and not too low,
     spread over with kusha grass, deer-skin, and a piece of cloth.

तत्रैकाग्रं मनः कृत्वा यतचित्तेन्द्रियक्रियः ।
उपविश्यासने युञ्ज्याद्योगमात्मविशुद्धये ॥ १२ ॥

समं कायशिरोग्रीवं धारयन्नचलं स्थिरः ।
संप्रेक्ष्य नासिकाग्रं स्वं दिशश्चानवलोकयन् ॥ १३ ॥

प्रशान्तात्मा विगतभीर्ब्रह्मचारिव्रते स्थितः ।
मनः संयम्य मच्चित्तो युक्त आसीत मत्परः ॥ १४ ॥

युञ्जन्नेवं सदात्मानं योगी नियतमानसः ।
शान्तिं निर्वाणपरमां मत्संस्थामधिगच्छति ॥ १५ ॥

नात्यश्रतस्तु योगोऽस्ति न चैकान्तमनश्रतः ।
न चाति स्वप्नशीलस्य जाग्रतो नैव चार्जुन ॥ १६ ॥

युक्ताहारविहारस्य युक्तचेष्टस्य कर्मसु ।
युक्तस्वप्नावबोधस्य योगो भवति दुःखहा ॥ १७ ॥

यदा विनियतं चित्तमात्मन्येवावतिष्ठते ।
निःस्पृहः सर्वकामेभ्यो युक्त इत्युच्यते तदा ॥ १८ ॥

यथा दीपो निवातस्थो नेङ्गते सोपमा स्मृता ।
योगिनो यतचित्तस्य युञ्जतो योगमात्मनः ॥ १९ ॥

यत्रोपरमते चित्तं निरुद्धं योगसेवया ।
यत्र चैवात्मनात्मानं पश्यन्नात्मनि तुष्यति ॥ २० ॥

सुखमात्यन्तिकं यत्तद्बुद्धिग्राह्यमतीन्द्रियम् ।
वेत्ति यत्र न चैवायं स्थितश्चलति तत्त्वतः ॥ २१ ॥

यं लब्ध्वा चापरं लाभं मन्यते नाधिकं ततः ।
यस्मिन्स्थितो न दुःखेन गुरुणापि विचाल्यते ॥ २२ ॥

तं विद्याद् दुःखसंयोगवियोगं योगसंज्ञितम् ।
स निश्चयेन योक्तव्यो योगोऽनिर्विण्णचेतसा ॥ २३ ॥ .

12   And, fixing his mind on a single goal, subduing the
         demands of the eager senses,
      he should struggle in Yoga, to cleanse his heart.

13   And he must hold his body still, his head and neck erect,
      not let his eyes stray, but gaze only at the tip of his nose.

14   Tranquil and courageous, an avowed brahmachari,
      his mind subdued, his thought focused on me, he must sit,
         considering me his ultimate goal.

15   Thus absorbed, thus steadfast, lost in me, he will find peace,
      and the bliss beyond peace, called Nirvana.

16   Yoga is not for the glutton, or one who fasts too much;
      it is not for the sleep-heavy or the sleepless.

17   Yoga destroys despair; it is only for the moderate
      in eating and resting, in sleeping and working.

18   You become tranquil when the subdued mind is established
         in the atman,
      when anxiety is overcome, and desires abandoned.

19   The flame of a windless lamp is never fitful —
      a good simile for a controlled yogi, absorbed in Yoga.

20   When the mind is steady in Yoga, and achieves tranquillity,
      and when the atman reveals Brahman, when one is
         contented in the atman;

21   When perfect calm comes, experienced by the liberated atman
      (a goal from which there is no straying);

22   And when, having achieved this ineffable state,
      no anxiety disturbs —

23   Yoga is won!
      And this is achieved after much hardship.

संकल्पप्रभवान्कामांस्त्यक्त्वा सर्वानशेषतः ।
मनसैवेन्द्रियग्रामं विनियम्य समन्ततः ॥ २४ ॥

शनैः शनैरुपरमेद्बुद्ध्या धृतिगृहीतया ।
आत्मसंस्थं मनः कृत्वा न किंचिदपि चिन्तयेत् ॥ २५ ॥

यतो यतो निश्चरति मनश्चञ्चलमस्थिरम् ।
ततस्ततो नियम्यैतदात्मन्येव वशं नयेत् ॥ २६ ॥

प्रशान्तमनसं ह्येनं योगिनं सुखमुत्तमम् ।
उपैति शान्तरजसं ब्रह्मभूतमकल्मषम् ॥ २७ ॥

युञ्जन्नेवं सदात्मानं योगी विगतकल्मषः ।
सुखेन ब्रह्मसंस्पर्शमत्यन्तं सुखमश्नुते ॥ २८ ॥

सर्वभूतस्थमात्मानं सर्वभूतानि चात्मनि ।
ईक्षते योगयुक्तात्मा सर्वत्र समदर्शनः ॥ २९ ॥

यो मां पश्यति सर्वत्र सर्वं च मयि पश्यति ।
तस्याहं न प्रणश्यामि स च मे न प्रणश्यति ॥ ३० ॥

सर्वभूतस्थितं यो मां भजत्येकत्वमास्थितः ।
सर्वथा वर्तमानोऽपि स योगी मयि वर्तते ॥ ३१ ॥

आत्मौपम्येन सर्वत्र समं पश्यति योऽर्जुन ।
सुखं वा यदि वा दुःखं स योगी परमो मतः ॥ ३२ ॥

अर्जुन उवाच

योऽयं योगस्त्वया प्रोक्तः साम्येन मधुसूदन ।
एतस्याहं न पश्यामि चञ्चलत्वात्स्थितिं स्थिराम् ॥ ३३ ॥

चञ्चलं हि मनः कृष्ण प्रमाथि बलवद्दृढम् ।
तस्याहं निग्रहं मन्ये वायोरिव सुदुष्करम् ॥ ३४ ॥

श्रीभगवानुवाच

असंशयं महाबाहो मनो दुर्निग्रहं चलम् ।
अभ्यासेन तु कौन्तेय वैराग्येण च गृह्यते ॥ ३५ ॥

असंयतात्मना योगो दुष्प्राप इति मे मतिः ।
वश्यात्मना तु यतता शक्योऽवाप्तुमुपायतः ॥ ३६ ॥

24   Forsaking desire, and controlling his senses,
      the yogi must not think of anything else.

25   Success will come by slow degrees.
      Should his fickle mind stray,

26   He must subdue it, reclaim it,
      and guide it by the atman.

27   The supreme bliss is found only by the tranquil yogi,
      whose passions have been stilled.

28   His desires washed away,
      the yogi easily achieves union with Brahman.

29   He sees the atman in all beings, and all being in the atman,
      for his heart is firm in Yoga.

30   Who sees me in all things, and all things in me,
      he is never far from me, and I am never far from him.

31   He worships me and lives in me, whoever he might be,
      for he has achieved unity of being, he sees me in all things.

32   He treats delight and suffering everywhere as his own,
      he is the supreme yogi.

33   Arjuna said:
      You have told me this Yoga of peace and unity of being,
      but my mind is restless, I do not understand what you say

34   For the mind Krishna is powerful, violent, uncontrollable.
      harnessing the mind is like harnessing the wind.

35   Krishna replied:
      The mind indeed is all that you say, Arjuna,
      but determination helps; and renunciation curbs it.

36   Without determination, no man can reach Yoga,
      but the self-disciplined, struggling nobly, can achieve it.

अर्जुन उवाच

अयतिः श्रद्धयोपेतो योगाच्चलितमानसः ।
अप्राप्य योगसंसिद्धिं कां गतिं कृष्ण गच्छति ॥ ३७ ॥

कच्चिन्नोभयविभ्रष्टश्छिन्नाभ्रमिव नश्यति ।
अप्रतिष्ठो महाबाहो विमूढो ब्रह्मणः पथि ॥ ३८ ॥

एतन्मे संशयं कृष्ण छेत्तुमर्हस्यशेषतः ।
त्वदन्यः संशयस्यास्य छेत्ता न ह्युपपद्यते ॥ ३९ ॥

श्रीभगवानुवाच

पार्थ नैवेह नामुत्र विनाशस्तस्य विद्यते ।
न हि कल्याणकृत्कश्चिद्दुर्गतिं तात गच्छति ॥ ४० ॥

प्राप्य पुण्यकृतां लोकानुषित्वा शाश्वतीः समाः ।
शुचीनां श्रीमतां गेहे योगभ्रष्टोऽभिजायते ॥ ४१ ॥

अथवा योगिनामेव कुले भवति धीमताम् ।
एतद्धि दुर्लभतरं लोके जन्म यदीदृशम् ॥ ४२ ॥

तत्र तं बुद्धिसंयोगं लभते पौर्वदेहिकम् ।
यतते च ततो भूयः संसिद्धौ कुरुनन्दन ॥ ४३ ॥

पूर्वाभ्यासेन तेनैव ह्रियते ह्यवशोऽपि सः ।
जिज्ञासुरपि योगस्य शब्दब्रह्मातिवर्तते ॥ ४४ ॥

प्रयत्नाद्यतमानस्तु योगी संशुद्धकिल्बिषः ।
अनेकजन्मसंसिद्धस्ततो याति परां गतिम् ॥ ४५ ॥

तपस्विभ्योऽधिको योगी ज्ञानिभ्योऽपि मतोऽधिकः ।
कर्मिभ्यश्चाधिको योगी तस्माद्योगी भवार्जुन ॥ ४६ ॥

योगिनामपि सर्वेषां मद्गतेनान्तरात्मना ।
श्रद्धावान्भजते यो मां स मे युक्ततमो मतः ॥ ४७ ॥

37 Arjuna asked:
    What happens to the well-meaning man who does not
        succeed in Yoga
    whose mind wanders, who loses control —

38 Does he not plummet down,
    is he not doomed like a tattered cloud?

39 Dispel this doubt, Krishna —
    you are the best remover of doubt.

40 Krishna replied:
    He need not fear, neither now nor later —
    the struggle for virtue is never wasted.

41 He reaches the worlds of the blessed, and lives a long time;
    then he is reincarnated in the homes of the prosperous and
        the righteous.

42 Or he finds birth among learned yogis —
    a difficult birth to obtain, very difficult.

43 There he gets back his former intelligence,
    and once again struggles in Yoga.

44 His primary struggle continues its momentum.
    Even a man who merely asks to be enlightened in Yoga
        is superior to the performer of mechanical rituals.

45 The yogi who perseveres,
    revolves through numerous births before reaching the
        supreme goal.

46 Be a yogi, Arjuna, for the yogi is above those who do penance,
    above the learned, and above the active workers.

47 And even among yogis, he is the best who communes with
        me in his atman.
    I am sure of this.

THE YOGA OF KNOWLEDGE

*S*ome truths have to be accepted by the novice in yoga as self-evident: selfishness harms, selflessness improves; there is a lower, pulling-down tendency in man's make-up, and there is a higher, raising-up movement as well; an invisible divine shakti holds the universes of the cosmos together, like pearls hanging on a string; life is an ambivalent mix of delight and disgust, right and wrong, high and low, progress and regress.

Though self-evident, these truths can be, and have to be, learnt, acquired, accepted, divined, taken on trust, gained by experience, intuition or symbiosis. Whichever way they come is fine, for they make special and precious the person who knows them. The key shloka of Canto VII is number 17: 'He is dear to me' (sa cha mama priyah). Of the four kinds of good people — the sorrowing, the seeker after truth, the seeker of bliss, and the wise — the wise is the best. The suffering person wishes to end his sorrow, the truth-seeker hopes to gain enlightenment, the seeker of bliss (some translate this as 'wealth') wants salvation. All are using talent or skill as a means to an end. Only the wise man is secure in the knowledge that wisdom is an end in itself. He has seen through the myriad fruit-offering seductions of maya. He is not deceived by the dangling carrots of sex, fame, money, and power; by the dazzling interplay of cause and effect. He knows that wisdom's lamp is self-glowing, self-secure, self-charging.

It is wisdom, says Krishna, to know the Adhyatman, the Adhibhuta, the Adhidaiva, and the Adhiyajna.

श्रीभगवानुवाच

मय्यासक्तमनाः पार्थ योगं युञ्जन्मदाश्रयः ।
असंशयं समग्रं मां यथा ज्ञास्यसि तच्छृणु ॥ १ ॥

ज्ञानं तेऽहं सविज्ञानमिदं वक्ष्याम्यशेषतः ।
यज्ज्ञात्वा नेह भूयोऽन्यज्ज्ञातव्यमवशिष्यते ॥ २ ॥

मनुष्याणां सहस्रेषु कश्चिद्यतति सिद्धये ।
यततामपि सिद्धानां कश्चिन्मां वेत्ति तत्त्वतः ॥ ३ ॥

भूमिरापोऽनलो वायुः खं मनो बुद्धिरेव च ।
अहंकार इतीयं मे भिन्ना प्रकृतिरष्टधा ॥ ४ ॥

अपरेयमितस्त्वन्यां प्रकृतिं विद्धि मे पराम् ।
जीवभूतां महाबाहो ययेदं धार्यते जगत् ॥ ५ ॥

एतद्योनीनि भूतानि सर्वाणीत्युपधारय ।
अहं कृत्स्नस्य जगतः प्रभवः प्रलयस्तथा ॥ ६ ॥

मत्तः परतरं नान्यत्किञ्चिदस्ति धनञ्जय ।
मयि सर्वमिदं प्रोतं सूत्रे मणिगणा इव ॥ ७ ॥

रसोऽहमप्सु कौन्तेय प्रभास्मि शशिसूर्ययोः ।
प्रणवः सर्ववेदेषु शब्दः खे पौरुषं नृषु ॥ ८ ॥

पुण्यो गन्धः पृथिव्यां च तेजश्चास्मि विभावसौ ।
जीवनं सर्वभूतेषु तपश्चास्मि तपस्विषु ॥ ९ ॥

बीजं मां सर्वभूतानां विद्धि पार्थ सनातनम् ।
बुद्धिर्बुद्धिमतामस्मि तेजस्तेजस्विनामहम् ॥ १० ॥

बलं बलवतां चाहं कामरागविवर्जितम् ।
धर्माविरुद्धो भूतेषु कामोऽस्मि भरतर्षभ ॥ ११ ॥

ये चैव सात्त्विका भावा राजसास्तामसाश्च ये ।
मत्त एवेति तान्विद्धि न त्वहं तेषु ते मयि ॥ १२ ॥

1   Krishna continued:
    Listen, Arjuna, to how you can come to me,
    by sheltering in me, and practising Yoga.

2   I will tell you all knowledge, all realization;
    after knowing which, there is nothing more to know.

3   Out of thousands one perhaps strives for perfection,
    and one perhaps out of those who strive actually finds me.

4   Earth, water, fire, air, ether;
    mind, intellect, and egoism — these eight constituents
        make up Nature.

5   This is the lower Nature but different from this is the
        higher Nature —
    the principle of life which sustains the worlds.

6   These two, womb of all life, are in my power;
    I am the birth and dissolution of this universe.

7   There is nothing superior to me, Arjuna:
    the worlds depend on me as pearls hang on a string.

8   I am the salt of the ocean, the brilliance of the moon and
        the sun,
    I am Om in the Vedas, and sound in the sky, and manliness
        in man.

9   I am fragrance in the earth, and brightness in fire:
    I am life in all, and penance in the pure ones.

10 Consider me the undying seed of all life:
    the glory of the glorious, the wisdom of the wise.

11 I am the pure and selfless strength of the strong:
    I am desire too, desire that does not transgress dharma.

12 They are all mine, the states of sattva, and rajas, and tamas;
    I am not in them: they are in me.

त्रिभिर्गुणमयैर्भावैरेभिः सर्वमिदं जगत् ।
मोहितं नाभिजानाति मामेभ्यः परमव्ययम् ॥ १३ ॥

दैवी ह्येषा गुणमयी मम माया दुरत्यया ।
मामेव ये प्रपद्यन्ते मायामेतां तरन्ति ते ॥ १४ ॥

न मां दुष्कृतिनो मूढाः प्रपद्यन्ते नराधमाः ।
माययापहृतज्ञाना आसुरं भावमाश्रिताः ॥ १५ ॥

चतुर्विधा भजन्ते मां जनाः सुकृतिनोऽर्जुन ।
आर्तो जिज्ञासुरर्थार्थी ज्ञानी च भरतर्षभ ॥ १६ ॥

तेषां ज्ञानी नित्ययुक्त एकभक्तिर्विशिष्यते ।
प्रियो हि ज्ञानिनोऽत्यर्थमहं स च मम प्रियः ॥ १७ ॥

उदाराः सर्व एवैते ज्ञानी त्वात्मैव मे मतम् ।
आस्थितः स हि युक्तात्मा मामेवानुत्तमां गतिम् ॥ १८ ॥

बहूनां जन्मनामन्ते ज्ञानवान्मां प्रपद्यते ।
वासुदेवः सर्वमिति स महात्मा सुदुर्लभः ॥ १९ ॥

कामैस्तैस्तैर्हृतज्ञानाः प्रपद्यन्तेऽन्यदेवताः ।
तं तं नियममास्थाय प्रकृत्या नियताः स्वया ॥ २० ॥

यो यो यां यां तनुं भक्तः श्रद्धयार्चितुमिच्छति ।
तस्य तस्याचलां श्रद्धां तामेव विदधाम्यहम् ॥ २१ ॥

स तया श्रद्धया युक्तस्तस्याराधनमीहते ।
लभते च ततः कामान्मयैव विहितान्हि तान् ॥ २२ ॥

अन्तवत्तु फलं तेषां तद्भवत्यल्पमेधसाम् ।
देवान्देवयजो यान्ति मद्भक्ता यान्ति मामपि ॥ २३ ॥

13   These three manifestations of the three gunas deceive the
         world,
      and it fails to recognize me, because I am beyond them.

14   It is difficult indeed to pierce this divine maya of the gunas.
      But the faithful are able to pierce it.

15   The ill-minded and the ignorant are victims of maya,
      and do not worship me.

16   There are four types of good men who worship me, Arjuna:
      the sorrowing, the truth-seeker, the seeker of bliss,
         and the wise man.

17   The wise man, steadfast, devoted to me, is the best among
         these.
      I love the wise, Arjuna, and he is dear to me.

18   They are all good, but the wise man is as my own self:
      his mind is balanced, he is devoted to me as the supreme
         goal.

19   After many births, the wise man reposes in me, convinced
         that I am all:
      such a pure soul is difficult to come across.

20   There are others, made blind by various desires,
      who adhere to various rites, prostrate themselves before
         various gods, according to their natures.

21   I make firm the devotion of any worshipper,
      no matter what his form of worship is.

22   And with that devotion he progresses in worship,
      and obtains his desires, which I alone offer.

23   But the reward for men of small intelligence is small.
      The worshippers of the gods go to the gods;
         who loves me comes to me.

अव्यक्तं व्यक्तिमापन्नं मन्यन्ते मामबुद्धयः ।
परं भावमजानन्तो ममाव्ययमनुत्तमम् ॥ २४ ॥

नाहं प्रकाशः सर्वस्य योगमायासमावृतः ।
मूढोऽयं नाभिजानाति लोको मामजमव्ययम् ॥ २५ ॥

वेदाहं समतीतानि वर्तमानानि चार्जुन ।
भविष्याणि च भूतानि मां तु वेद न कश्चन ॥ २६ ॥

इच्छाद्वेषसमुत्थेन द्वन्द्वमोहेन भारत ।
सर्वभूतानि संमोहं सर्गे यान्ति परंतप ॥ २७ ॥

येषां त्वन्तगतं पापं जनानां पुण्यकर्मणाम् ।
ते द्वन्द्वमोहनिर्मुक्ता भजन्ते मां दृढव्रताः ॥ २८ ॥

जरामरणमोक्षाय मामाश्रित्य यतन्ति ये ।
ते ब्रह्म तद्विदुः कृत्स्नमध्यात्मं कर्म चाखिलम् ॥ २९ ॥

साधिभूताधिदैवं मां साधियज्ञं च ये विदुः ।
प्रयाणकालेऽपि च मां ते विदुर्युक्तचेतसः ॥ ३० ॥

24   I am formless. but the foolish think I have form.
      They do not understand my real nature.

25   I am covered by maya, and all do not see me.
      I am birthless and deathless.
          This world of illusion does not understand me.

26   I know what is, what was, and what will be;
      but none knows me.

27   The play of ambivalence, of disgust and delight,
      flings all beings into delusion.

28   But holy men free themselves from extremes,
      and become my devoted worshippers.

29   They strive for salvation from death and old age,
          they shelter in me;
      they understand Brahman and the nature of karma.

30   They continue in knowledge till the time of death, for they
          are firm of reason:
      they know the Adhibhuta, the Adhidaiva, the Adhiyajna,
          and the Adhyatman.

THE NATURE OF BRAHMAN

*A*dhyatman, Adhibhuta, Adhidaiva, Adhiyajna: this quartet constitutes the quintessence of natural and supernatural knowledge which, intelligently filtered in a receptive mind, becomes wisdom.

Adhyatman (adhi-atman: pervader of the atman). Adhibhuta (pervader of all creatures). Adhidaiva (pervader of the gods). Adhiyajna (pervader of ritual deeds).

Behind the technical philosophical terminology, the meaning is clear. The Supreme Ultimate Brahman is the energizing principle behind the individual atman, the Fire, of which the atman is a spark. Brahman also energizes the vast variety of physical life. Brahman charges the creative imagination of the morally noble and god-like. Brahman inspires the dedicated selflessness that goes into ritual acts such as sacred offerings and sacrifices. The key shloka 15 of Canto VIII applies to a person who has this wisdom: 'For such a pure soul (mahatma) there is no more the sorrow of rebirth.'

No commentator has satisfactorily glossed the two shlokas that speak of Time that makes yogis return to the world (by the dark path) and not return (by the bright path). Perhaps fire, brilliance, daytime, the bright fortnight and the six-month course of the northern sun refers to the mystic insights into one pole of the ambivalence of maya. The opposite pole of the dark path might refer to the insights of occult, or tantric, 'wisdom' — the dark side of ambivalence which ensures not salvation (moksha) but re-birth.

अर्जुन उवाच

किं तद्ब्रह्म किमध्यात्मं किं कर्म पुरुषोत्तम ।
अधिभूतं च किं प्रोक्तमधिदैवं किमुच्यते ॥ १ ॥

अधियज्ञ: कथं कोऽत्र देहेऽस्मिन्मधुसूदन ।
प्रयाणकाले च कथं ज्ञेयोऽसि नियतात्मभि: ॥ २ ॥

श्री भगवानुवाच

अक्षरं ब्रह्म परमं स्वभावोऽध्यात्ममुच्यते।
भूतभावोद्भवकरो विसर्ग: कर्मसंज्ञित: ॥ ३ ॥

अधिभूतं क्षरो भाव: पुरुषश्चाधिदैवतम् ।
अधियज्ञोऽहमेवात्र देहे देहभृतां वर ॥ ४ ॥

अन्तकाले च मामेव स्मरन्मुक्त्वा कलेवरम् ।
य: प्रयाति स मद्भावं याति नास्त्यत्र संशय: ॥ ५ ॥

यं यं वापि स्मरन्भावं त्यजत्यन्ते कलेवरम् ।
तं तमेवैति कौन्तेय सदा तद्भावभावित: ॥ ६ ॥

तस्मात्सर्वेषु कालेषु मामनुस्मर युध्य च ।
मय्यर्पितमनोबुद्धिर्मामेवैष्यस्यसंशयम् ॥ ७ ॥

अभ्यासयोगयुक्तेन चेतसा नान्यगामिना ।
परमं पुरुषं दिव्यं याति पार्थानुचिन्तयन् ॥ ८ ॥

कविं पुराणमनुशासितारमणोरणीयांसमनुस्मरेद्य: ।
सर्वस्य धातारमचिन्त्यरूपमादित्यवर्णं तमस: परस्तात् ॥ ९ ॥

प्रयाणकाले मनसाचलेन
    भक्त्या युक्तो योगबलेन चैव ।
भ्रुवोर्मध्ये प्राणमावेश्य सम्यक्
    स तं परं पुरुषमुपैति दिव्यम् ॥ १० ॥

1   Arjuna asked:
     Purushottama, what is Brahman, and Adhyatman, and Karma?
     What is Adhibhuta, and what is Adhidaiva?

2   And what is Adhiyajna and how?
     And how will the self-restrained realize you, at the time
          of death?

3   Krishna replied:
     Brahman is the Supreme Indestructible, and its existence
          in separate persons is Adhyatman.
     Karma is the momentum that commences the birth of beings.

4   The destructible is Adhibhuta, and the male principle is
          Adhidaiva,
     and I am Adhiyajna in the human body.

5   He attains my being, abandoning his body,
          whose oncentration at the time of death is on me.
     Do not doubt this.

6   Whatever his concentration is on,
     he achieves that at the time of death.

7   Therefore, think of me —and fight!
     Your meditation focused on me, you shall achieve me.

8   Absolutely unwavering, consistently absorbed
          in the male principle, the Purusha,
     the mind reaches him.

9   'The Purusha is all-knowing, lord of all, the ancient,
          smaller than an atom, incomprehensible of form,
     dazzling as the sun, and free of the veiling darkness of maya.'

10   He achieves Purusha who, at the time of death, is steady
          and devoted;
     has fixed his life-breath through the power of Yoga
          between his eyebrows, and who thinks thus.

यदक्षरं वेदविदो वदन्ति
विशन्ति यद्यतयो वीतरागाः ।
यदिच्छन्तो ब्रह्मचर्यं चरन्ति
तत्ते पदं संग्रहेण प्रवक्ष्ये ॥ ११ ॥

सर्वद्वाराणि संयम्य मनो हृदि निरुध्य च ।
मूर्ध्न्याधायात्मनः प्राणमास्थितो योगधारणाम् ॥ १२ ॥

ओमित्येकाक्षरं ब्रह्म व्याहरन्मामनुस्मरन् ।
यः प्रयाति त्यजन्देहं स याति परमां गतिम् ॥ १३ ॥

अनन्यचेताः सततं यो मां स्मरति नित्यशः ।
तस्याहं सुलभः पार्थ नित्ययुक्तस्य योगिनः ॥ १४ ॥

मामुपेत्य पुनर्जन्म दुःखालयमशाश्वतम् ।
नापुवन्ति महात्मानः संसिद्धिं परमां गताः ॥ १५ ॥

आब्रह्मभुवनाल्लोकाः पुनरावर्तिनोऽर्जुन ।
मामुपेत्य तु कौन्तेय पुनर्जन्म न विद्यते ॥ १६ ॥

सहस्त्रयुगपर्यन्तमहर्यद्ब्रह्मणो विदुः ।
रात्रिं युगसहस्त्रान्तां तेऽहोरात्रविदो जनाः ॥ १७ ॥

अव्यक्ताद्व्यक्तयः सर्वाः प्रभवन्त्यहरागमे ।
रात्र्यागमे प्रलीयन्ते तत्रैवाव्यक्तसंज्ञके ॥ १८ ॥

भूतग्रामः स एवायं भूत्वा भूत्वा प्रलीयते ।
रात्र्यागमेऽवशः पार्थ प्रभवत्यहरागमे ॥ १९ ॥

परस्तस्मात्तु भावोऽन्योऽव्यक्तोऽव्यक्तात्सनातनः ।
यः स सर्वेषु भूतेषु नश्यत्सु न विनश्यति ॥ २० ॥

अव्यक्तोऽक्षर इत्युक्तस्तमाहुः परमां गतिम् ।
यं प्राप्य न निवर्तन्ते तद्धाम परमं मम ॥ २१ ॥

11 I will now tell you of what the learned in the Vedas
        conceive as the Imperishable,
    which is achieved through the self-control of brahmacharya.

12 With his senses all restrained,
    absorbed in yogic meditation,

13 He achieves the supreme goal,
    who forsakes his body with the syllable Om on his lips,
        symbol of Brahman.

14 The yogi who every day keeps me in mind,
    constant and steadfast, finds me easy of achievement.

15 He reaches the supreme perfection, and he achieves me;
    for such a pure soul there is no more the sorrow of rebirth.

16 Even the world of Brahma cannot escape rebirth;
    but there is no rebirth once I am achieved.

17 The man who understands day and night can also
        understand the thousand-yuga day of Brahma
    and his thousand-yuga night.

18 When the day of Brahma commences, all forms evolve
        from the unmanifested;
    when night commences, they dissolve into the unmanifested.

19 And this swarm of beings, successively reborn, dissolves
        as the night of Brahma commences,
    and emerges with the commencement of another day.

20 But beyond this unmanifested,
        there is another Unmanifested, the undying reality,
    which does not dissolve though all beings dissolve.

21 This Indestructible and Unmanifested is the Supreme Goal:
    this is Brahman; this is the state of perfection from which
        there is no rebirth.

पुरुषः स परः पार्थ भक्त्या लभ्यस्त्वनन्यया ।
यस्यान्तःस्थानि भूतानि येन सर्वमिदं ततम् ॥ २२ ॥

यत्र काले त्वनावृत्तिमावृत्तिं चैव योगिनः ।
प्रयाता यान्ति तं कालं वक्ष्यामि भरतर्षभ ॥ २३ ।'

अग्निर्ज्योतिरहः शुक्रः षण्मासा उत्तरायणम् ।
तत्र प्रयाता गच्छन्ति ब्रह्म ब्रह्मविदो जनाः ॥ २४ ॥

धूमो रात्रिस्तथा कृष्णः षण्मासा दक्षिणायनम् ।
तत्र चान्द्रमसं ज्योतिर्योगी प्राप्य निवर्तते ॥ २५ ॥

शुक्लकृष्णे गती ह्येते जगतः शाश्वते मते ।
एकया यात्यनावृत्तिमन्ययावर्तते पुनः ॥ २६ ॥

नैते सृती पार्थ जानन्योगी मुह्यति कश्चन ।
तस्मात्सर्वेषु कालेषु योगयुक्तो भवार्जुन ॥ २७ ॥

वेदेषु यज्ञेषु तपःसु चैव
     दानेषु यत्पुण्यफलं प्रदिष्टम् ।
अत्येति तत्सर्वमिदं विदित्वा
     योगी परं स्थानमुपैति चाद्यम् ॥ २८ ॥

22   Only complete worship of him in whom all things repose,
     of him who pervades all the worlds,
         can obtain this supreme perfection.

23   I will tell you of time which makes yogis return to the world,
     and not return.

24   Fire, brilliance, daytime, the bright fortnight, and the
         six-month course of the northern sun —
     this takes the knowers of Brahman to Brahman.

25   Smoke, night-time, the dark fortnight, and the six-month
         course of the southern sun —
     this takes the yogi to the lunar brilliance, but he returns.

26   Rightly are they thought absolute, these bright and dark
         paths:
     for one results in non-return; the other causes return.

27   The yogi who understands the nature of these paths is not
         deceived;
     therefore, Arjuna, make yourself firm in Yoga.

28   For the yogi is above the rewards offered in the Vedas,
         above ritual, penance and charity —
     he alone understands the nature of Reality,
         he alone finds the supreme goal.

THE SECRET OF WORK

*L*ogic and reason and discussion, Socratic dialogue and Vyasan question-and-answer go as far as the limits set by the human brain. At a certain point, the queries stop, the imagination falters, the heart remains unsatisfied. The conviction is partial not total, because the analytic method has not been fulfilled by the mystic vision and intuitive insight.

'The worlds hang on me like pearls on a string' — was Krishna's poetic metaphor to suggest a mystical truth. He proceeds further now by saying, 'My invisible presence straddles this universe.....' Like the invisible wind reposing in the sky, 'all beings repose in me'. He is referring to the 'yogamaishvaram,' the miraculous Yoga by which the invisible informs the visible, the transcendent permeates the physical, the divine irradiates the secular, while remaining 'neutral, unattached', unbound (nibadhna). Inapprehensible, we clutch Thee!

The key shloka of Canto IX is number 23: 'Even the worshippers of images, in reality worship me; their faith (shraddha) is real, though their means is poor.'

It is a magical word: shraddha. The closest English equivalent is 'faith'. But shraddha has associations with darshan, and worshipping a physical image of a non-physical divinity is a form of darshan provided it is done with shraddha. No shraddha is refused: 'I will accept any gift, a fruit, a flower, a leaf, even water, if it is offered purely, and devoutly, with love.... No worshipper of mine is ever rejected.'

श्रीभगवानुवाच

इदं तु ते गुह्यतमं प्रवक्ष्याम्यनसूयवे ।
ज्ञानं विज्ञानसहितं यज्ज्ञात्वा मोक्ष्यसेऽशुभात् ॥ १ ॥

राजविद्या राजगुह्यं पवित्रमिदमुत्तमम् ।
प्रत्यक्षावगमं धर्म्यं सुसुखं कर्तुमव्ययम् ॥ २ ॥

अश्रद्धानाः पुरुषा धर्मस्यास्य परंतप ।
अप्राप्य मां निवर्तन्ते मृत्युसंसारवर्त्मनि ॥ ३ ॥

मया ततमिदं सर्वं जगदव्यक्तमूर्तिना ।
मत्स्थानि सर्वभूतानि न चाहं तेष्ववस्थितः ॥ ४ ॥

न च मत्स्थानि भूतानि पश्य मे योगमैश्वरम् ।
भूतभृन्न च भूतस्थो ममात्मा भूतभावनः ॥ ५ ॥

यथाकाशस्थितो नित्यं वायुः सर्वत्रगो महान् ।
तथा सर्वाणि भूतानि मत्स्थानीत्युपधारय ॥ ६ ॥

सर्वभूतानि कौन्तेय प्रकृतिं यान्ति मामिकाम् ।
कल्पक्षये पुनस्तानि कल्पादौ विसृजाम्यहम् ॥ ७ ॥

प्रकृतिं स्वामवष्टभ्य विसृजामि पुनः पुनः ।
भूतग्राममिमं कृत्स्नमवशं प्रकृतेर्वशात् ॥ ८ ॥

न च मां तानि कर्माणि निबध्नन्ति धनञ्जय ।
उदासीनवदासीनमसक्तं तेषु कर्मसु ॥ ९ ॥

मयाध्यक्षेण प्रकृतिः सूयते सचराचरम् ।
हेतुनानेन कौन्तेय जगद्विपरिवर्तते ॥ १० ॥

1   Krishna continued:
      I will give you the profoundest of secrets, Arjuna,
      leading to perfection, for you are not cynical.

2   This is the most perfect of sciences, of secrets the most
            profound, of salvations the supreme;
      this you will understand immediately, and perform without
            difficulty.

3   Disrespectful men, ignoring this, fail to attain me,
      and fall into fearful rebirths.

4   My invisible presence straddles this Universe:
      all beings have life in me, but I am not in them.

5   Look at my miraculous Yoga, Arjuna —even beings are not
            in me!
      Though it creates and sustains beings, my Self is not
            established in them.

6   Like the tremendous wind reposing in the sky though it
            seems to travel everywhere,
      so all beings repose in me.

7   And when a day of Brahma ends, all beings return to my
            Nature;
      when a day begins, they emerge again.

8   I vitalize my Prakriti, and this swarm of beings is evolved,
      all subordinate to Prakriti.

9   But these acts do not affect me, Arjuna —
      I am neutral, unattached.

10   Under my supervision, Nature turns out the animate and
            the inanimate;
      this is the reason the world forever keeps spinning.

अवजानन्ति मां मूढा मानुषीं तनुमाश्रितम् ।
परं भावमजानन्तो मम भूतमहेश्वरम् ॥ ११ ॥

मोघाशा मोघकर्माणो मोघज्ञाना विचेतसः ।
राक्षसीमासुरीं प्रकृतिं मोहिनीं श्रिताः ॥ १२ ॥

महात्मानस्तु मां पार्थ दैवीं प्रकृतिमाश्रिताः ।
भजन्त्यनन्यमनसो ज्ञात्वा भूतादिमव्ययम् ॥ १३ ॥

सततं कीर्तयन्तो मां यतन्तश्च दृढव्रताः ।
नमस्यन्तश्च मां भक्तया नित्ययुक्ता उपासते ॥ १४ ॥

ज्ञानयज्ञेन चाप्यन्ये यजन्तो मामुपासते ।
एकत्वेन पृथक्त्वेन बहुधा विश्वतोमुखम् ॥ १५ ॥

अहं क्रतुरहं यज्ञः स्वधाहमहमौषधम् ।
मन्त्रोऽहमहमेवाज्यमहमग्निरहं हुतम् ॥ १६ ॥

पिताहमस्य जगतो माता धाता पितामहः ।
वेद्यं पवित्रमोङ्कार ऋक्साम यजुरेव च ॥ १७ ॥

गतिर्भर्ता प्रभुः साक्षी निवासः शरणं सुहृत् ।
प्रभवः प्रलयः स्थानं निधानं बीजमव्ययम् ॥ १८ ॥

तपाम्यहमहं वर्षं निगृह्णाम्युत्सृजामि च ।
अमृतं चैव मृत्युश्च सदसच्चाहमर्जुन ॥ १९ ॥

त्रैविद्या मां सोमपाः पूतपापा
    यज्ञैरिष्ट्वा स्वर्गतिं प्रार्थयन्ते ।
ते पुण्यमासाद्य सुरेन्द्रलोक-
    मश्नन्ति दिव्यान्दिवि देवभोगान् ॥ २० ॥

11   The ignorant fail to recognize me in my human form,
      because they are not aware of my status as lord of all beings.

12   Hollow of hopes, hollow of deeds, hollow of knowledge,
      they are like rakshasas, swamped by delusions.

13   But the mahatmas have knowledge of my transcendent nature:
      they consider me the changeless source of being, they
            adore me with single-minded devotion.

14   They worship me, and they sing my praises;
      they strive resolutely for me; they pay homage to me, they
            are always constant.

15   Others worship me as the all-formed, as unity,
      as many-formed, as separate: each worships as best as he can.

16   I am the ritual, the sacred gift, and the sacred tree,
      I am the holy food, and the mantra, I am the sacred fire
            and the sacred offering.

17   I am the father and mother of this world, I maintain it
            and purify it;
      I am the goal of knowledge, I am Om and the three Vedas;

18   The supporter, the refuge, the lord, the silent witness, the
            friend,
      the origin, the dissolution, the storehouse, and the seed.

19   I offer heat: I send and withhold rain:
      I am death and moksha, Arjuna:
            I am what is, I am what is not.

20   The learned in the three Vedas worship me and drink the
            soma juice, and, purified, they pray for heaven;
      reaching the world of Indra, they enjoy the pleasures of
            the gods.

ते तं भुक्त्वा स्वर्गलोकं विशालं
क्षीणे पुण्ये मर्त्यलोक विशन्ति ।
एवं त्रयीधर्ममनुप्रपन्ना
गतागतं कामकामा लभन्ते ॥ २१ ॥

अनन्याश्चिन्तयन्तो मां ये जनाः पर्युपासते ।
तेषां नित्याभियुक्तानां योगक्षेमं वहाम्यहम् ॥ २२ ॥

येऽप्यन्यदेवता भक्ता यजन्ते श्रद्धयान्विताः ।
तेऽपि मामेव कौन्तेय यजन्त्यविधिपूर्वकम् ॥ २३ ॥

अहं हि सर्वयज्ञानां भोक्ता च प्रभुरेव च ।
न तु मामभिजानन्ति तत्त्वेनातश्च्यवन्ति ते ॥ २४ ॥

यान्ति देवव्रता देवान्पितृन्यान्ति पितृव्रताः ।
भूतानि यान्ति भूतेज्या यान्ति मद्याजिनोऽपि माम् ॥ २५ ॥

पत्रं पुष्पं फलं तोयं यो मे भक्त्या प्रयच्छति ।
तदहं भक्त्युपहृतमश्रामि प्रयतात्मनः ॥ २६ ॥

यत्करोषि यदश्रासि यज्जुहोषि ददासि यत् ।
यत्तपस्यसि कौन्तेय तत्कुरुष्व मदर्पणम् ॥ २७ ॥

शुभाशुभफलैरेवं मोक्ष्यसे कर्मबन्धनैः ।
संन्यासयोगयुक्तात्मा विमुक्तो मामुपैष्यसि ॥ २८ ॥

समोऽहं सर्वभूतेषु न मे द्वेष्योऽस्ति न प्रियः ।
ये भजन्ति तु मां भक्त्या मयि ते तेषु चाप्यहम् ॥ २९ ॥

अपि चेत्सुदुराचारो भजते मामनन्यभाक् ।
साधुरेव स मन्तव्यः सम्यग्व्यवसितो हि सः ॥ ३० ॥

21   Having enjoyed heaven, they return to the material world
        because their virtues have been sufficiently rewarded.
      Those who adhere to the words of the Vedas are doomed
        to constant rebirth.

22   But those who worship me and my unity in all beings are
        the truly persevering,
      and to these I give what they do not have and increase
        what they have.

23   Even the worshippers of images, in reality worship me;
      their faith is real, though their means are poor.

24   For I am the lord and enjoyer of all ritual;
      but because they do not know me, they are born again.

25   The worshippers of the gods achieve the gods; of the fathers,
        the fathers;
      the worshippers of the spirits go to the spirits;
        my worshippers come to me.

26   I will accept any gift, a fruit, a flower, a leaf, even water,
      if it is offered purely, and devoutly, and with love.

27   Whatever you do, Arjuna, whatever you sacrifice,
      whatever you give in charity, whatever penance you
        perform, do it for my sake.

28   This will free you from the fetters of work,
      and you will come to me, with your heart steady in Yoga.

29   All beings are the same to me, Arjuna:
      I hate none, I love none; but those who are my devoted
        worshippers, they are in me, and I am in them.

30   If the wickedest man acknowledges me as supreme above
        all, regard him virtuous, Arjuna:
      he has chosen the true path.

क्षिप्रं भवति धर्मात्मा शश्वच्छान्तिं निगच्छति ।
कौन्तेय प्रतिजानीहि न मे भक्तः प्रणश्यति ॥ ३१ ॥

मां हि पार्थ व्यपाश्रित्य येऽपि स्युः पापयोनयः ।
स्त्रियो वैश्यास्तथा शूद्रास्तेऽपि यान्ति परां गतिम् ॥ ३२ ॥

किं पुनर्ब्राह्मणाः पुण्या भक्ता राजर्षयस्तथा ।
अनित्यमसुखं लोकमिमं प्राप्य भजस्व माम् ॥ ३३ ॥

मन्मना भव मद्भक्तो मद्याजी मां नमस्कुरु ।
मामेवैष्यसि युक्त्वैवमात्मानं मत्परायणः ॥ ३४ ॥

31   Soon will he become pure-hearted, and achieve undying
         peace.
      I promise you this: no worshipper of mine is ever rejected.

32   Sheltering in me,
      all achieve the supreme goal —
      women, Vaishyas, Shudras, and all of low birth.

33   Small wonder then that pious Brahmins and steadfast saints
         find me.
      Give up this brief joyless world, Arjuna, and strive for me.

34   Be in me, Arjuna. Worship me. Sacrifice to me.
      Bow to me. And so you will come to me.

THE UNIVERSAL GLORY

W*hat faith provides is an experience that reason can only indicate or describe: the 'divine glories' (divyanam vibhutanam) and 'unfathomable prowess' (vibhutervistaro) of Godhead. That is why the key shlokas of Canto X are numbers 40 and 42, specially 42: 'What use to you is this parade of my powers? —Have faith in me; know I exist, and that I sustain the world.'*

Connected with shraddha (faith) is bhakti (devotion). Bhakti, because it is outgoing, is the very opposite of desire, which is in-growing and so, when faith and devotion join hands, compassion is born. 'My compassion like a glowing; lamp of wisdom scatters the ignorant darkness' of any who happily sing the glories of God.

Arjuna's problem is obvious. As a Kshatriya warrior, he is unfamiliar with the coordinates of bhakti, though he knows what shraddha is, since training in arms under a guru demands the strictest shraddha. The only way he can discover the meaning of bhakti is by asking what it is — a very poor way — as unhelpful as trying to experience the fragrance of a rose by looking up its definition in a dictionary.

Yet Krishna goes along with Arjuna's request for a 'narration' of his yoga-vibhuti. How Arjuna will get a taste of this bhakti nectar (amrita: non-death) will become clear as the narration continues. The ladder of reason is a prelude to the leap of faith and devotion.

श्रीभगवानुवाच

भूय एव महाबाहो शृणु मे परमं वचः ।
यत्तेऽहं प्रीयमाणाय वक्ष्यामि हितकाम्यया ॥ १ ॥

न मे विदुः सुरगणाः प्रभवं न महर्षयः ।
अहमादिर्हि देवानां महर्षीणां च सर्वशः ॥ २ ॥

यो मामजमनादिं च वेत्ति लोकमहेश्वरम् ।
असंमूढः स मर्त्येषु सर्वपापैः प्रमुच्यते ॥ ३ ॥

बुद्धिर्ज्ञानमसंमोहः क्षमा सत्यं दमः शमः ।
सुखं दुःखं भवोऽभावो भयं चाभयमेव च ॥ ४ ॥

अहिंसा समता तुष्टिस्तपो दानं यशोऽयशः ।
भवन्ति भावा भूतानां मत्त एव पृथग्विधाः ॥ ५ ॥

महर्षयः सप्त पूर्वे चत्वारो मनवस्तथा ।
मद्भावा मानसा जाता येषां लोक इमाः प्रजाः ॥ ६ ॥

एतां विभूतिं योगं च मम यो वेत्ति तत्त्वतः ।
सोऽविकम्पेन योगेन युज्यते नात्र संशयः ॥ ७ ॥

अहं सर्वस्य प्रभवो मत्तः सर्वं प्रवर्तते ।
इति मत्वा भजन्ते मां बुधा भावसमन्विताः ॥ ८ ॥

मच्चित्ता मद्गतप्राणा बोधयन्तः परस्परम् ।
कथयन्तश्च मां नित्यं तुष्यन्ति च रमन्ति च ॥ ९ ॥

तेषां सततयुक्तानां भजतां प्रीतिपूर्वकम् ।
ददामि बुद्धियोगं तं येन मामुपयान्ति ते ॥ १० ॥

1   Krishna continued:
    Listen to my wisdom, Arjuna:
    I speak for your good, for you are a good listener.

2   Neither the gods nor the saints have understood my divine
        origin;
    for I am the cause of the birth of the gods and the saints.

3   Whoever knows me as birthless, without beginning, and
        the supreme master of the universe,
    he of all mortals sees clear, and is absolved of taint.

4   Intellect, knowledge, vision, perseverance, truth and
        renunciation,
    gentleness, joy, sorrow, birth, death, awe, fearlessness,

5   Ahimsa, equanimity, penance and charity, fame and sense
        of shame —
    these human states arise from my being alone.

6   The seven saints and the four founders of the human race
        were products of my mind;
    from them was born this swarm of life.

7   This is the truth.
    The man who knows the difference between illusion and
        reality is the yogi.

8   I am the source of everything,
        everything evolves from me —
    thinking in this manner,
        the learned concentrate on me.

9   Their minds in me, their senses in me,
    instructing each other and singing my glory,
        they are happy.

10 And I enlighten them, and they come to me,
    for they are devoted and steadfast.

तेषामेवानुकम्पार्थमहमज्ञानजं तमः ।
नाशयाम्यात्मभावस्थो ज्ञानदीपेन भास्वता ॥ ११ ॥

अर्जुन उवाच

परं ब्रह्म परं धाम पवित्रं परमं भवान् ।
पुरुषं शाश्वतं दिव्यमादिदेवमजं विभुम् ॥ १२ ॥

आहुस्त्वामृषयः सर्वे देवर्षिर्नारदस्तथा ।
असितो देवलो व्यासः स्वयं चैव ब्रवीषि मे ॥ १३ ॥

सर्वमेतदृतं मन्ये यन्मां वदसि केशव ।
न हि ते भगवन्व्यक्तिं विदुर्देवा न दानवाः ॥ १४ ॥

स्वयमेवात्मनात्मानं वेत्थ त्वं पुरुषोत्तम ।
भूतभावन भूतेश देवदेव जगत्पते ॥ १५ ॥

वक्तुमर्हस्यशेषेण दिव्या ह्यात्मविभूतयः ।
याभिर्विभूतिभिर्लोकानिमांस्त्वं व्याप्य तिष्ठसि ॥ १६ ॥

कथं विद्यामहं योगिंस्त्वां सदा परिचिन्तयन् ।
केषु केषु च भावेषु चिन्त्योऽसि भगवन्मया ॥ १७ ॥

विस्तरेणात्मनो योगं विभूतिं च जनार्दन ।
भूयः कथय तृप्तिर्हि शृण्वतो नास्ति मेऽमृतम् ॥ १८ ॥

श्रीभगवानुवाच

हन्त ते कथयिष्यामि दिव्या ह्यात्मविभूतयः ।
प्राधान्यतः कुरुश्रेष्ठ नास्त्यन्तो विस्तरस्य मे ॥ १९ ॥

अहमात्मा गुडाकेश सर्वभूताशयस्थितः ।
अहमादिश्च मध्यं च भूतानामन्त एव च ॥ २० ॥

आदित्यानामहं विष्णुर्ज्योतिषां रविरंशुमान् ।
मरीचिर्मरुतामस्मि नक्षत्राणामहं शशी ॥ २१ ॥

11 I dwell in their heart,
    and my compassion like a glowing lamp of wisdom scatters
        their ignorant darkness.

12 Arjuna said:
    You are the Supreme Brahman, the supreme goal, the
        supreme purifier;
    self-glowing Purusha, the first God;

13 Narada, Asita, Devala, and Vyasa have called you eternal,
    and this is now your own revelation.

14 All that you say to me is true, Krishna;
    neither the gods nor the anti-gods comprehend your essence.

15 You alone know yourself by yourself, transcendent Purusha;
    you are the source of life, the God of gods, the Lord of
        the world.

16 Speak to me of your divine powers which sustain the world
    and proclaim your existence.

17 How shall I achieve you, Krishna?
    What shall be the objects of my meditation?

18 Narrate your Yoga and your glory at length.
    Such nectar from your lips is what I desire.

19 Krishna replied:
    I shall narrate you my divine glories in a brief sequence —
    there is no end otherwise to them.

20 I am the atman, conscious in the heart of all life;
    and I am also the beginning, the middle, and the end of
        all life.

21 I am the Vishnu of the Adityas, the glorious sun among
        heavenly bodies;
    Marichi among the winds, and the moon among planets.

वेदानां सामवेदोऽस्मि देवानामस्मि वासवः ।
इन्द्रियाणां मनश्चास्मि भूतानामस्मि चेतना ॥ २२ ॥

रुद्राणां शंकरश्चास्मि वित्तेशो यक्षरक्षसाम् ।
वसूनां पावकश्चास्मि मेरुः शिखरिणामहम् ॥ २३ ॥

पुरोधसां च मुख्यं मां विद्धि पार्थ बृहस्पतिम् ।
सेनानीनामहं स्कन्दः सरसामस्मि सागरः ॥ २४ ॥

महर्षीणां भृगुरहं गिरामस्म्येकमक्षरम् ।
यज्ञानां जपयज्ञोऽस्मि स्थावराणां हिमालयः ॥ २५ ॥

अश्वत्थः सर्ववृक्षाणां देवर्षीणां च नारदः ।
गन्धर्वाणां चित्ररथः सिद्धानां कपिलो मुनिः ॥ २६ ॥

उच्चैःश्रवसमश्वानां विद्धि माममृतोद्भवम् ।
ऐरावतं गजेन्द्राणां नराणां च नराधिपम् ॥ २७ ॥

आयुधानामहं वज्रं धेनूनामस्मि कामधुक् ।
प्रजनश्चास्मि कन्दर्पः सर्पाणामस्मि वासुकिः ॥ २८ ॥

अनन्तश्चास्मि नागानां वरुणो यादसामहम् ।
पितृणामर्यमा चास्मि यमः संयमतामहम् ॥ २९ ॥

प्रह्लादश्चास्मि दैत्यानां कालः कलयतामहम् ।
मृगाणां च मृगेन्द्रोऽहं वैनतेयश्च पक्षिणाम् ॥ ३० ॥

पवनः पवतामस्मि रामः शस्त्रभृतामहम् ।
झषाणां मकरश्चास्मि स्रोतसामस्मि जाह्नवी ॥ ३१ ॥

22   Of the Vedas I am Samaveda, Indra among gods;
      of the faculties I am intelligence; and I am the
         consciousness of the world's creatures.

23   I am Shankara among the Rudras and Kubera among the
         Yakshas and Rakshasas;
      I am Pavaka among the Vasus, and among mountains I
         am Meru.

24   Among priests, Arjuna, I am Brihaspati,
      among commanders Skanda, and the ocean among
         expanses of water.

25   I am Bhrigu among saints, Om among words,
      among sacrifices I am Japayajna, and the Himalaya among
         steadfast objects.

26   Among trees I am the fig-tree, and Narada among holy men,
      among Gandharvas Chitraratha, and Kapila among saints.

27   Among horses I am Ucchaishravas, sprung from nectar;
      among elephants Airavata, and among human beings king.

28   Among weapons I am the thunderbolt, and among cattle
         the heavenly cow:
      I am sexual desire too, creator of life; and among snakes I
         am Vasuki.

29   Ananta among serpents, Varuna among creatures of the sea;
      the Aryaman of spirits of fathers, and the god of death
         among governors;

30   Prahlada of Daityas, Kala of measures,
      lion among beasts, Garuda among birds;

31   Among cleansers I am the wind, Parashurama among
         warriors,
      the crocodile among fish, the Ganga among rivers.

सर्गाणामादिरन्तश्च मध्यं चैवाहमर्जुन ।
अध्यात्मविद्या विद्यानां वादः प्रवदतामहम् ॥ ३२ ॥

अक्षराणामकारोऽस्मि द्वन्द्वः सामासिकस्य च ।
अहमेवाक्षयः कालो धाताहं विश्वतोमुखः ॥ ३३ ॥

मृत्युः सर्वहरश्चाहमुद्भवश्च भविष्यताम् ।
कीर्तिः श्रीर्वाक्च नारीणां स्मृतिर्मेधा धृतिः क्षमा ॥ ३४ ॥

बृहत्साम तथा साम्नां गायत्री छन्दसामहम् ।
मासानां मार्गशीर्षोऽहमृतूनां कुसुमाकरः ॥ ३५ ॥

द्यूतं छलयतामस्मि तेजस्तेजस्विनामहम् ।
जयोऽस्मि व्यवसायोऽस्मि सत्त्वं सत्त्ववतामहम् ॥ ३६ ॥

वृष्णीनां वासुदेवोऽस्मि पाण्डवानां धनञ्जयः ।
मुनीनामप्यहं व्यासः कवीनामुशना कविः ॥ ३७ ॥

दण्डो दमयतामस्मि नीतिरस्मि जिगीषताम् ।
मौनं चैवास्मि गुह्यानां ज्ञानं ज्ञानवतामहम् ॥ ३८ ॥

यच्चापि सर्वभूतानां बीजं तदहमर्जुन ।
न तदस्ति विना यत्स्यान्मया भूतं चराचरम् ॥ ३९ ॥

नान्तोऽस्ति मम दिव्यानां विभूतीनां परंतप ।
एष तूद्देशतः प्रोक्तो विभूतेर्विस्तरो मया ॥ ४० ॥

यद्यद्विभूतिमत्सत्त्वं श्रीमदूर्जितमेव वा ।
तत्तदेवावगच्छ त्वं मम तेजोंऽशसंभवम् ॥ ४१ ॥

अथवा बहुनैतेन किं ज्ञातेन तवार्जुन ।
विष्टभ्याहमिदं कृत्स्नमेकांशेन स्थितो जगत् ॥ ४२ ॥

32   I am the beginning, the middle and the end of all that is flux;
among wisdoms I am knowledge of the atman, and I am
truth among disputes.

33   Among letters I am A, among compounds the Dvandva;
I am immeasurable Kala, and the many-formed sustainer.

34   I am merciless death, I am the wealth of the wealthy;
among female virtues I am fame, beauty, memory, wisdom,
chastity, and sweet speech.

35   Among hymns I am Brihatsama, among metres the Gayatri;
among months Margashirsh and among seasons spring full
of flowers;

36   I am the deceit of the deceitful, and the strength of the strong;
I am struggle, I am realization, and the virtue of the virtuous.

37   I am Krishna among the Yadavas, and Arjuna among the
Pandavas;
among poets I am Vyasa, among ascetics Ushanas.

38   Among punishers I am the mace;
I am the subtlety of the tactful, the silence of the secretive,
and the wisdom of the wise.

39   I am the germ of life;
nothing animate or inanimate has existence without me.

40   There is no limit to my divine glory,
this is but a fragment you hear of my unfathomable prowess.

41   If there is any man powerful, blessed and talented,
his glory is derived from a part of my glory.

42   But what use to you is this parade of my powers?
Have faith in me; know I exist, and that I sustain the worlds.

THE COSMIC MULTI-REVELATION

*C*anto XI is the vishva-rupa-darshan, *the mystic cosmic multi-revelation of Divinity. To some, it is the pinnacle of the* Gita, *the poem's dazzling hard-core truth, its quintessence. To others, it is a betrayal of confidence, with Krishna stunning Arjuna with magic when all that Arjuna wanted was logic. To each his own. What matters is that the Canto flows naturally and effortlessly out of Canto X. The stepping stone of reason has led to the threshold of faith. What Arjuna 'sees' is nothing less than everything: birth/death, creation/dissolution, Kala the preserver and Kala the destroyer, Krishna calamitous and Krishna compassionate. He had earlier begged Krishna not to 'bewilder' him with confusing speech: 'Tell me that one truth (tadekam vada) by which I may know you.' This then is that one truth, simultaneously freeing and fearful, a horripilating experience of the unity that underlies the multitudinosity of reality.*

The key shloka of Canto XI cannot be any but number 12: 'Were a thousand suns to explode suddenly in the sky, their brilliance would approximate the glory of the sight.' This shloka was quoted in its entirety by E.Robert Oppenheimer when the first nuclear device was exploded in the Nevada desert (Oppenheimer had studied Sanskrit in his college days)

The 'beatific' vision brings a sea-change in Arjuna, and he asks no more questions. Prostrating himself before Krishna in total anjali, he receives the rest of the Gita with a newly discovered spiritual humility.

अर्जुन उवाच

मदनुग्रहाय परमं गुह्यमध्यात्मसंज्ञितम् ।
यत्त्वयोक्तं वचस्तेन मोहोऽयं विगतो मम ॥ १ ॥

भवाप्ययौ हि भूतानां श्रुतौ विस्तरशो मया ।
त्वत्तः कमलपत्राक्ष माहात्म्यमपि चाव्ययम् ॥ २ ॥

एवमेतद्यथात्थ त्वमात्मानं परमेश्वर ।
द्रष्टुमिच्छामि ते रूपमैश्वरं पुरुषोत्तम ॥ ३ ॥

मन्यसे यदि तच्छक्यं मया द्रष्टुमिति प्रभो ।
योगेश्वर ततो मे त्वं दर्शयात्मानमव्ययम् ॥ ४ ॥

श्रीभगवानुवाच

पश्य मे पार्थ रूपाणि शतशोऽथ सहस्रशः ।
नानाविधानि दिव्यानि नानावर्णाकृतीनि च ॥ ५ ॥

पश्यादित्यान्वसून्रुद्रानश्विनौ मरुतस्तथा ।
बहून्यदृष्टपूर्वाणि पश्याश्चर्याणि भारत ॥ ६ ॥

इहैकस्थं जगत्कृत्स्नं पश्याद्य सचराचरम् ।
मम देहे गुडाकेश यच्चान्यद्द्रष्टुमिच्छसि ॥ ७ ॥

न तु मां शक्यसे द्रष्टुमनेनैव स्वचक्षुषा ।
दिव्यं ददामि ते चक्षुः पश्य मे योगमैश्वरम् ॥ ८ ॥

सञ्जय उवाच

एवमुक्त्वा ततो राजन्महायोगेश्वरो हरिः ।
दर्शयामास पार्थाय परमं रूपमैश्वरम् ॥ ९ ॥

अनेकवक्त्रनयनमनेकाद्भुतदर्शनम् ।
अनेकदिव्याभरणं दिव्यानेकोद्यतायुधम् ॥ १० ॥

दिव्यमाल्याम्बरधरं दिव्यगन्धानुलेपनम् ।
सर्वाश्चर्यमयं देवमनन्तं विश्वतोमुखम् ॥ ११ ॥

1   Arjuna said:
      You have destroyed my doubts with your compassionate
          words,
      full of wisdom about the nature of Brahman.

2   I have heard of your greatness,
      I have heard of the birth and death of creatures.

3   And there is truth in your words, O Parameshvara!
      I ask you, Purushottama, give me revelation!

4   If you think me worthy, Krishna,
      I beg of you, Yogeshvara, give me revelation!

5   Krishna said:
      Look, Arjuna, at my divine forms,
      various-coloured, various-shaped,
          in a bewildering panorama.

6   See the Adityas, and the Vasus, the Rudras, the Ashvins
          and the Maruts;
      see also glories you have never witnessed before.

7   See the entire universe revolving in me, the animate and the
          inanimate —
      see whatever else you wish to see.

8   I will grant you super-sensuous sight to witness my glory —
      your mortal eyes are unable to behold it.

9   Sanjaya reported:
      Then Krishna the Lord of yoga revealed
      his supreme form —

10   Possessing numerous mouths and eyes,
      glittering with divine ornaments, displaying divine signs,

11   Divinely garlanded, divinely scented,
      all-shaped, all-powerful, transcendent and limitless.

दिवि सूर्यसहस्रस्य भवेद्युगपदुत्थिता ।
यदि भाः सदृशी सा स्याद्भासस्तस्य महात्मनः ॥ १२ ॥

तत्रैकस्थं जगत्कृत्स्नं प्रविभक्तमनेकधा ।
अपश्यद्देवदेवस्य शरीरे पाण्डवस्तदा ॥ १३ ॥

ततः स विस्मयाविष्टो हृष्टरोमा धनञ्जयः ।
प्रणम्य शिरसा देवं कृताञ्जलिरभाषत ॥ १४ ॥

अर्जुन उवाच

पश्यामि देवांस्तव देव देहे सर्वांस्तथाभूतविशेषसङ्घान् ।
ब्रह्माणमीशं कमलासनस्थमृषींश्च सर्वानुरगाश्च दिव्यान् ॥ १५ ॥

अनेकबाहूदरवक्त्रनेत्रं पश्यामि त्वां सर्वतोऽनन्तरूपम् ।
नान्तं न मध्यं न पुनस्तवादिं पश्यामि विश्वेश्वर विश्वरूप ॥ १६ ॥

किरीटिनं गदिनं चक्रिणं च तेजोराशिं सर्वतो दीप्तिमन्तम् ।
पश्यामि त्वां दुर्निरीक्ष्यं समन्ताद्दीप्तानलार्कद्युतिमप्रमेयम् ॥ १७ ॥

त्वमक्षरं परमं वेदितव्यं त्वमस्य विश्वस्य परं निधानम् ।
त्वमव्ययः शाश्वतधर्मगोप्ता सनातनस्त्वं पुरुषो मतो मे ॥ १८ ॥

अनादिमध्यान्तमनन्तवीर्य-
          मनन्तबाहुं शशिसूर्यनेत्रम् ।
पश्यामि त्वां दीप्तहुताशवक्त्रं
          स्वतेजसा विश्वमिदं तपन्तम् ॥ १९ ॥

द्यावापृथिव्योरिदमन्तरं हि
          व्याप्तं त्वयैकेन दिशश्च सर्वाः ।
दृष्ट्वाद्भुतं रूपमुग्रं तवेदं
          लोकत्रयं प्रव्यथितं महात्मन् ॥ २० ॥

अमी हि त्वां सुरसङ्घा विशन्ति
          केचिद्भीताः प्राञ्जलयो गृणन्ति ।
स्वस्तीत्युक्त्वा महर्षिसिद्धसङ्घाः
          स्तुवन्ति त्वां स्तुतिभिः पुष्कलाभिः ॥ २१ ॥

12   Were a thousand suns to explode suddenly in the sky,
      their brilliance would approximate the glory of the sight.

13   And in the body of Krishna,
      Arjuna saw the separate universes united, and resting.

14   Struck with awe, his hair on end, horripilating,
      he bent his head, and offered pranama.

15   Arjuna said:
      I see all the gods in your body,
          O Vishveshvara, all variety of life.
      I see Brahma on the lotus, the saints, and the nagas.

16   I see your form stretching on every side, arms, stomachs,
          mouths and eyes,
      without beginning, middle, or end.

17   I see your crown, your chakra, your mace,
      your gathered radiance covering the three worlds.

18   You are the supreme reality,
          the end of knowledge;
      the shelter of the three worlds, the protector of dharma,
          the ancient Purusha.

19   I see you without start or growth or end, many-armed,
          omnipotent.
      The sun and the moon are your eyes, the flame in your
          mouth burns the three worlds.

20   You fill the interworld space and all things else;
      I shake with fear, the three worlds shake, witnessing your
          awesome form.

21   These countless gods merge into you, singing your praise
          with palms joined;
      Svasti! Prosper! is the chant of the saints and the yogis.

रूद्रादित्या वसवो ये च साध्या विश्वेऽश्विनौ मरुतश्चोष्मपाश्च ।
गन्धर्वयक्षासुरसिद्धसङ्घा वीक्षन्ते त्वां विस्मिताश्चैव सर्वे ॥ २२ ॥

रूपं महत्ते बहुवक्त्रनेत्रं महाबाहो बहुबाहूरुपादम् ।
बहूदरं बहुदंष्ट्राकरालं दृष्ट्वा लोकाः प्रव्यथितास्तथाहम् ॥ २३ ॥

नभःस्पृशं दीप्तमनेकवर्णं व्यात्ताननं दीप्तविशालनेत्रम् ।
दृष्ट्वा हि त्वां प्रव्यथितान्तरात्मा
       धृतिं न विन्दामि शमं च विष्णो ॥ २४ ॥

दंष्ट्राकरालानि च ते मुखानि दृष्ट्वैव कालानलसन्निभानि ।
दिशो न जाने न लभे च शर्म प्रसीद देवेश जगन्निवास ॥ २५ ॥

अमी च त्वां धृतराष्ट्रस्य पुत्राः सर्वे सहैवावनिपालसङ्घैः ।
भीष्मो द्रोणः सूतपुत्रस्तथासौ सहास्मदीयैरपि योधमुख्यैः ॥ २६ ॥

वक्त्राणि ते त्वरमाणा विशन्ति दंष्ट्राकरालानि भयानकानि ।
केचिद्विलग्ना दशनान्तरेषु संदृश्यन्ते चूर्णितैरुत्तमाङ्गैः ॥ २७ ॥

यथा नदीनां बहवोऽम्बुवेगाः समुद्रमेवाभिमुखा द्रवन्ति ।
तथा तवामी नरलोकवीरा विशन्ति वक्त्राण्यभिविज्वलन्ति ॥ २८ ॥

यथा प्रदीप्तं ज्वलनं पतङ्गा
       विशन्ति नाशाय समृद्धवेगाः ।
तथैव नाशाय विशन्ति लोका-
       स्तवापि वक्त्राणि समृद्धवेगाः ॥ २९ ॥

लेलिह्यसे ग्रसमानः समन्ता-
       ल्लोकान्समग्रान्वदनैर्ज्वलद्भिः ।
तेजोभिरापूर्य जगत्समग्रं
       भासस्तवोग्राः प्रतपन्ति विष्णो ॥ ३० ॥

आख्याहि मे को भवानुग्ररूपो
       नमोऽस्तु ते देववर प्रसीद ।
विज्ञातुमिच्छामि भवन्तमाद्यं
       न हि प्रजानामि तव प्रवृत्तिम् ॥ ३१ ॥

22   The Rudras, the Adityas, the Vasus, the Ashvins, the
          Maruts, the Gandharvas, the Yakshas,
       the anti-gods and the Siddhas — all marvel,
          all are spellbound.

23   Seeing your limitless form, many-mouthed, many-eyed,
          many-armed,
       many-thighed, -bellied, and -footed, the worlds are
          spellbound, and I am spellbound.

24   I see you reach the sky, glorious with colour, with mouths
          agape, and wide red eyes, and my heart knows fear,
          my steadfastness disappears:
       O Krishna, peace deserts me.

25   Take pity, O God, Lord of the three worlds.
       Seeing your mouths, vivid with teeth glowing like fires on
          the day of dissolution,
          my head whirls. O Krishna, peace has deserted me.

26   Bhishma, Drona and Karna,
       Dhritarashtra's sons, kings and warriors,

27   Sweep into your mouth;
       between your teeth their heads protrude,
          dreadfully crushed.

28   Like many small streams rushing to the ocean,
       these heroes rush into your flaming mouths.

29   Like moths rushing to the fatal flame,
       these heroes rush into your flaming mouths.

30   And you chew the worlds in your flaming mouths, and
          lick your lips;
       O Krishna, your shafts of flame brighten the universe.

31   Tell me who you are, O fiery-formed.
       O Krishna, have pity. How can I know you?

श्री भगवानुवाच

कालोऽस्मि लोकक्षयकृत्प्रवृद्धो लोकान्समाहर्तुमिह प्रवृत्तः ।
ऋतेऽपि त्वां न भविष्यन्ति सर्वे
       येऽवस्थिताः प्रत्यनीकेषु योधाः ॥ ३२ ॥

तस्मात्त्वमुत्तिष्ठ यशो लभस्व
       जित्वा शत्रून्भुङ्क्ष्व राज्यं समृद्धम् ।
मयैवैते निहताः पूर्वमेव निमित्तमात्रं भव सव्यसाचिन् ॥ ३३ ॥

द्रोणं च भीष्मं च जयद्रथं च कर्णं तथान्यानपि योधवीरान् ।
मया हतांस्त्वं जहि मा व्यथिष्ठा
       युध्यस्व जेतासि रणे सपत्नान् ॥ ३४ ॥

सञ्जय उवाच

एतच्छ्रुत्वा वचनं केशवस्य कृताञ्जलिर्वेपमानः किरीटी ।
नमस्कृत्वा भूय एवाह कृष्णं सगद्गदं भीतभीतः प्रणम्य ॥ ३५ ॥

अर्जुन उवाच

स्थाने हृषीकेश तव प्रकीर्त्या जगत्प्रहृष्यत्यनुरज्यते च ।
रक्षांसि भीतानि दिशो द्रवन्ति सर्वे नमस्यन्ति च सिद्धसङ्घाः ॥ ३६ ॥

कस्माच्च ते न नमेरन्महात्मन् गरीयसे ब्रह्मणोऽप्यादिकर्त्रे ।
अनन्त देवेश जगन्निवास त्वमक्षरं सदसत्तत्परं यत् ॥ ३७ ॥

त्वमादिदेवः पुरुषः पुराणस्त्वमस्य विश्वस्य परं निधानम् ।
वेत्तासि वेद्यं च परं च धाम त्वया ततं विश्वमनन्तरूप ॥ ३८ ॥

वायुर्यमोऽग्निर्वरुणः शशाङ्कः प्रजापतिस्त्वं प्रपितामहश्च ।
नमो नमस्तेऽस्तु सहस्रकृत्वः पुनश्च भूयोऽपि नमो नमस्ते ॥ ३९ ॥

नमः पुरस्तादथ पृष्ठतस्ते
       नमोऽस्तु ते सर्वत एव सर्व ।
अनन्तवीर्यामितविक्रमस्त्वं
       सर्वं समाप्नोषि ततोऽसि सर्वः ॥ ४० ॥

32   Krishna replied:
     I am Time, Kala, supreme destroyer of the three worlds,
          here visible in the three worlds.
     Even if you refuse to fight, none of these soldiers will live.

33   Wake up, Arjuna, and win glory! Destroy your enemies
          and enjoy their kingdom!
     Their death is ordained — you are only the immediate cause.

34   All have already been killed by me —
     Drona and Bhishma, Jayadratha, Karna and the others.
          Fight! the day is yours.

35   Sanjaya reported:
     Hearing this, Arjuna, shaking,
     prostrated himself before Krishna.

36   Arjuna said:
     It is in the fitness of things, Krishna, that the world rejoices
          and sings your praises, the rakshasas scatter in fear,
     and bands of devotees stand in silent supplication.

37   Why shouldn't they? Why shouldn't they worship the
          creator of Brahma, the lord of Brahma, the Infinite,
          the God of gods, the refuge of the three worlds?
     You are deathless, you are real, your are unreal,
          you are what is beyond these.

38   You are the first God, and the primal Purusha, the refuge
          of the three worlds, the knower and the known,
          the ultimate end.
     O Infinite Form, the universe is rich with you!

39   You are the god of wind, fire, and death, you, are Prajapati;
     I worship you a thousand times, and a thousand times again.

40   May homage flow to you from all quarters!
     Your boundless power sweeps the universe. You are all.

सखेति मत्वा प्रसभं यदुक्तं हे कृष्ण हे यादव हे सखेति ।
अजानता महिमानं तवेदं मया प्रमादात्प्रणयेन वापि ॥ ४१ ॥

यच्चावहासार्थमसत्कृतोऽसि विहारशय्यासनभोजनेषु ।
एकोऽथवाप्यच्युत तत्समक्षं तत्क्षामये त्वामहमप्रमेयम् ॥ ४२ ॥

पितासि लोकस्य चराचरस्य त्वमस्य पूज्यश्च गुरुर्गरीयान् ।
न त्वत्समोऽस्त्यभ्यधिकः कुतोऽन्यो
लोकत्रयेऽप्यप्रतिमप्रभाव ॥ ४३ ॥

तस्मात्प्रणम्य प्रणिधाय कायं प्रसादये त्वामहमीशमीड्यम् ।
पितेव पुत्रस्य सखेव सख्युः प्रियः प्रियायार्हसि देव सोढुम् ॥ ४४ ॥

अदृष्टपूर्वं हृषितोऽस्मि दृष्ट्वा भयेन च प्रव्यथितं मनो मे ।
तदेव मे दर्शय देवरूपं प्रसीद देवेश जगन्निवास ॥ ४५ ॥

किरीटिनं गदिनं चक्रहस्तमिच्छामि त्वां द्रष्टुमहं तथैव ।
तेनैव रूपेण चतुर्भुजेन सहस्रबाहो भव विश्वमूर्ते ॥ ४६ ॥

श्रीभगवानुवाच

मया प्रसन्नेन तवार्जुनेदं रूपं परं दर्शितमात्मयोगात् ।
तेजोमयं विश्वमनन्तमाद्यं यन्मे त्वदन्येन न दृष्टपूर्वम् ॥ ४७ ॥

न वेदयज्ञाध्ययनैर्न दानैर्न च क्रियाभिर्न तपोभिरुग्रैः ।
एवंरूपः शक्य अहं नृलोके द्रष्टुं त्वदन्येन कुरुप्रवीर ॥ ४८ ॥

मा ते व्यथा मा च विमूढभावो दृष्ट्वा रूपं घोरमीदृङ्ममेदम् ।
व्यपेतभीः प्रीतमनाः पुनस्त्वं तदेव मे रूपमिदं प्रपश्य ॥ ४९ ॥

सञ्जय उवाच

इत्यर्जुनं वासुदेवस्तथोक्त्वा
स्वकं रूपं दर्शयामास भूयः ।
आश्वासयामास च भीतमेनं
भूत्वा पुनः सौम्यवपुर्महात्मा ॥ ५० ॥

41   And I have presumed, from love and casual regard, and
          called you Krishna, Yadava, and friend,
       thinking you a friend, unmindful of your glory.

42   I have lowered you in laughter, in resting, eating and walking,
       alone and in company. Forgive me, Krishna.

43   For you are the world's father, the goal of its supplication,
          the most mighty.
       The three worlds do not know your equal —who can
          surpass you?

44   I bend my body to your glory, and I beg forgiveness of
          you, my lord!
       Be merciful to me, as friend to friend, lover to beloved,
          father to son.

45   Though terror shudders in my heart, my joy brims over.
       O refuge of the worlds, O God of gods, I beg your grace.
       Reveal to me your form!

46   Let me see you with crown, mace, and chakra.
       I long to see you! O thousand-armed, show me your four-
          armed form!

47   Krishna said:
       My love shows you this supreme revelation, Arjuna;
       none has seen this before.

48   Neither study of the Vedas, sacrifices, gifts, ceremonies,
       nor the strictest penance will reveal me in this form to any
          other person.

49   Forget your fear and bewilderment.
       Throw off your terror, be glad of heart —and look!

50   Sanjaya reported:
       Krishna graced Arjuna with a vision of his peaceful form.
       Krishna gave Arjuna peace.

अर्जुन उवाच

दृष्ट्वेदं मानुषं रूपं तव सौम्यं जनार्दन ।
इदानीमस्मि संवृत्तः सचेताः प्रकृतिं गतः ॥ ५१ ॥

श्रीभगवानुवाच

सुदुर्दर्शमिदं रूपं दृष्ट्वानसि यन्मम ।
देवा अप्यस्य रूपस्य नित्यं दर्शनकाङ्क्षिणः ॥ ५२ ॥

नाहं वेदैर्न तपसा न दानेन न चेज्यया ।
शक्य एवंविधो द्रष्टुं दृष्ट्वानसि मां यथा ॥ ५३ ॥

भक्त्या त्वनन्यया शक्य अहमेवंविधोऽर्जुन ।
ज्ञातुं द्रष्टुं च तत्त्वेन प्रवेष्टुं च परंतप ॥ ५४ ॥

मत्कर्मकृन्मत्परमो मद्भक्तः सङ्गवर्जितः।
निर्वैरः सर्वभूतेषु यः स मामेति पाण्डव ॥ ५५ ॥

51   Arjuna said:
       Seeing your peaceful form, Krishna,
       my peace returns, I am normal again.

52   Krishna said:
       It is very difficult to see what you have seen;
       even the gods hunger for such a vision.

53   Neither the Vedas nor penance, charity, nor sacrifice,
       can make men see me as you have seen me.

54   Single-minded devotion alone
       can make this form of mine appear.

55   He reaches me who struggles for me,
       who has me as an ideal,
           who is free from desire and is unaffected by anger.

THE WAY OF DEVOTION

*S*raddha and bhakti — faith
and devotion — are the two words repeatedly stressed in the previous
two Cantos. The key last shloka of Canto XII clinches the favoured status
of devoted believers: 'Dear to me are those who walk along this deathless
dharma, and follow me with shraddha. They are my devotees, and I
love them.'

So far, in seven consecutive shlokas, 13-19, Krishna has described
the good points in the character of an ideal devotee (bhakta): compassion
for all creatures; absence of egotism; patience, fortitude; equanimity;
freedom from jealousy, fear and worry; self-sufficiency; indifference to
ups and downs; self-control, determination, decisiveness; impartiality
to friend and foe; equal-mindedness in devotion praise and blame;
silence, satisfaction; single-mindedness in devotion. At the end of each
sloka, he remarks: 'sa me priyah' (he is dear to me).

In the final shloka of the Canto, he adds, 'bhaktaste-ativa me
priyah'. 'Ativa priyah' ('exceedingly dear') — the only way one can
express it in English is by using the word 'love'. 'I love such devotees', is
what Krishna is saying. A stage has now been reached in the relationship
between confused Arjuna and confident Krishna when their Nara-
Narayana closeness asserts itself. This intimacy is very special. Arjuna
has been described by Krishna as his 'sakha' (a word for which there is
no parallel in English, though 'loving friend and loved friend' comes
near); and now Arjuna is on the brink of becoming a still more special
person: a sakha-bhakta, a loved and loving friend-cum-devotee.

अर्जुन उवाच

एवं सततयुक्ता ये भक्तास्त्वां पर्युपासते ।
ये चाप्यक्षरमव्यक्तं तेषां के योगवित्तमाः ॥ १ ॥

श्रीभगवानुवाच

मय्यावेश्य मनो ये मां नित्ययुक्ता उपासते ।
श्रद्धया परयोपेतास्ते मे युक्ततमा मताः ॥ २ ॥

ये त्वक्षरमनिर्देश्यमव्यक्तं पर्युपासते ।
सर्वत्रगमचिन्त्यं च कूटस्थमचलं ध्रुवम् ॥ ३ ॥

संनियम्येन्द्रियग्रामं सर्वत्र समबुद्धयः ।
ते प्राप्नुवन्ति मामेव सर्वभूतहिते रताः ॥ ४ ॥

क्लेशोऽधिकतरस्तेषामव्यक्तासक्तचेतसाम् ।
अव्यक्ता हि गतिर्दुःखं देहवद्भिरवाप्यते ॥ ५ ॥

ये तु सर्वाणि कर्माणि मयि संन्यस्य मत्पराः ।
अनन्येनैव योगेन मां ध्यायन्त उपासते ॥ ६ ॥

तेषामहं समुद्धर्ता मृत्युसंसारसागरात् ।
भवामि नचिरात्पार्थ मय्यावेशितचेतसाम् ॥ ७ ॥

मय्येव मन आधत्स्व मयि बुद्धिं निवेशय ।
निवसिष्यसि मय्येव अत ऊर्ध्वं न संशयः ॥ ८ ॥

अथ चित्तं समाधातुं न शक्नोषि मयि स्थिरम् ।
अभ्यासयोगेन ततो मामिच्छासुं धनञ्जय ॥ ९ ॥

अभ्यासेऽप्यसमर्थोऽसि मत्कर्मपरमो भव ।
मदर्थमपि कर्माणि कुर्वन्सिद्धिमवाप्स्यसि ॥ १० ॥

अथैतदप्यशक्तोऽसि कर्तुं मद्योगमाश्रितः ।
सर्वकर्मफलत्यागं ततः कुरू यतात्मवान् ॥ ११ ॥

1   Arjuna asked:
Who are the better yogis, Krishna, those who steadfastly
     worship you,
or those who worship the invisible and ineffable Brahman?

2   Krishna replied:
Those who worship me single-mindedly and those who
     have unshakable faith,
are for me the most learned in Yoga.

3   But those who worship the deathless Brahman,
the imperishable, unnameable, the invisible, the immutable,
     unshakable, and eternal —

4   They subdue their senses,
and seek the welfare of all, they also finally find me.

5   But their problems are greater:
for finite beings to attain the infinite is difficult.

6   Those who worship me,
offer their deeds to me, consider me the supreme goal,

7   And think of me with singleminded devotion —
I am their salvation from the whirlpool of the world.

8   Put all your mind in me, all your intelligence in me;
and you will certainly live in me for all time.

9   If you are unable to do so,
at least learn the importance of virtuous habit.

10   If the art of good habit is difficult,
learn to do everything for my sake —
     even that will suffice.

11   If even that is difficult, take shelter in me, do not hanker
     for the fruits of your actions.
Discipline yourself.

श्रेयो हि ज्ञानमभ्यासाज्ज्ञानाद्ध्यानं विशिष्यते ।
ध्यानात्कर्मफलत्यागस्त्यागाच्छान्तिरनन्तरम् ॥ १२ ॥

अद्वेष्टा सर्वभूतानां मैत्रः करूण एव च ।
निर्ममो निरहंकारः समदुःखसुखः क्षमी ॥ १३ ॥

संतुष्ट सततं योगी यतात्मा दृढनिश्चयः ।
मय्यर्पितमनोबुद्धिर्यो मद्भक्तः स मे प्रियः ॥ १४ ॥

यस्मान्नोद्विजते लोको लोकान्नोद्विजते च यः ।
हर्षामर्षभयोद्वेगैर्मुक्तो यः स च मे प्रियः ॥ १५ ॥

अनपेक्षः शुचिर्दक्ष उदासीनो गतव्यथः ।
सर्वारम्भपरित्यागी यो मद्भक्तः स मे प्रियः ॥ १६ ॥

यो न हृष्यति न द्वेष्टि न शोचति न काङ्क्षति ।
शुभाशुभपरित्यागी भक्तिमान्यः स मे प्रियः ॥ १७ ॥

समः शत्रौ च मित्रे च तथा मानापमानयोः ।
शीतोष्णसुखदुःखेषु समः सङ्गविवर्जितः ॥ १८ ॥

तुल्यनिन्दास्तुतिर्मौनी संतुष्टो येन केनचित् ।
अनिकेतः स्थिरमतिर्भक्तिमान्मे प्रियो नरः ॥ १९ ॥

ये तु धर्म्यामृतमिदं यथोक्तं पर्युपासते ।
श्रद्धाना मत्परमा भक्तास्तेऽतीव मे प्रियाः ॥ २० ॥

12   Knowledge is superior to good habit,
         meditation is superior to knowledge,
      and giving up the fruits of actions is superior to meditation.

13   Dear to me is the man who hates no one, who feels for all
         creatures,
      who has shed 'I' and 'mine', who is not excited by sorrow
         or joy,

14   Who is patient and serene,
      steadfast and subdued.

15   Dear to me is the man who neither annoys nor gets annoyed,
      who is free from passion, jealousy, fear and worry.

16   Dear to me is the man who is self-sufficient,
      chaste, indifferent, determined and decisive.

17   Dear to me is the man neither regretful nor passionate,
      who forsakes the fruits of deeds, renounces purity and
         impurity, and is devoted.

18   Dear to me is the man alike to friend and foe, alike in fame
         and infamy,
      in heat and cold, in joy and sorrow; unattached,

19   Equal-minded in blame or praise, silent, satisfied,
         undisturbed, singleminded in devotion.
      He is dear to me.

20   Dear to me are those who walk along this deathless
         dharma, and follow me with shraddha.
      They are my devotees, and I love them.

THE FIELD AND THE KNOWER OF THE FIELD

*I*t is to such a loved and loving
devotee that Krishna now offers insights into two of the subtlest concepts
of Upanishadic philosophy: Purusha and Prakriti, and Kshetra and
Kshetrajna. Loosely, one may translate the first pair as Male and Female;
or Spirit and Nature; or Soul and Matter; or Energy and Mass. The
second can be Englished with greater precision: Field and Knower of
the Field.

Purusha informs, permeates, energizes, and shines through
Prakriti. Prakriti is primordial, undifferentiated nature. Under the
spiritual influence of Purusha, Prakriti produces the universe, the raw
and refined, teeming, variegated life of the cosmos. However, Purusha,
the activating agent, itself remains unaffected. Like the sky that spreads
everywhere, Purusha (or Brahman or, in differentiated form, the
atman) remains pure. Paradoxically, though involved in Prakriti,
Purusha is the detached, supreme witness. It is not a participant.

Another way of looking at it is to describe Prakriti, in its
differentiated form, as the Kshetra, the Field, the Body, the Ground of
Karma's Fruits. The Kshetrajna is the knower of the Body, the atman,
the Witness, the Uninvolved Participant, the Bird Watching the Bird
Eating, always pure, always free, so long as it knows the truth about
itself and Prakriti. The key shloka 18 hymns this truth: 'It is the light of
lights, shining through darkness, it is the only knowledge worth knowing;
it is the end of knowledge; it exists in everyone's heart.'

अर्जुन उवाच

प्रकृतिं पुरुषं चैव क्षेत्रं क्षेत्रज्ञमेव च ।
एतद्वेदितुमिच्छामि ज्ञानं ज्ञेयं मतं मम ॥ १ ॥

श्रीभगवानुवाच

इदं शरीरं कौन्तेय क्षेत्रमित्यभिधीयते ।
एतद्यो वेत्ति तं प्राहुः क्षेत्रज्ञ इति तद्विदः ॥ २ ॥

क्षेत्रज्ञं चापि मां विद्धि सर्वक्षेत्रेषु भारत ।
क्षेत्रक्षेत्रज्ञयोर्ज्ञानं यत्तज्ज्ञानं मतं मम ॥ ३ ॥

तत्क्षेत्रं यच्च यादृक् च यद्विकारि यतश्च यत् ।
स च यो यत्प्रभावश्च तत्समासेन मे शृणु ॥ ४ ॥

ऋषिभिर्बहुधा गीतं छन्दोभिर्विविधैः पृथक् ।
ब्रह्मसूत्रपदैश्चैव हेतुमद्भिर्विनिश्चितैः ॥ ५ ॥

महाभूतान्यहंकारो बुद्धिरव्यक्तमेव च ।
इन्द्रियाणि दशैकं च पञ्च चेन्द्रियगोचराः ॥ ६ ॥

इच्छा द्वेषः सुखं दुःखं संघातश्चेतना धृतिः ।
एतत्क्षेत्रं समासेन सविकारमुदाहृतम् ॥ ७ ॥

अमानित्वमदम्भित्वमहिंसा क्षान्तिरार्जवम् ।
आचार्योपासनं शौच स्थैर्यमात्मविनिग्रहः ॥ ८ ॥

इन्द्रियार्थेषु वैराग्यमनहंकार एव च ।
जन्ममृत्युजराव्याधिदुःखदोषानुदर्शनम् ॥ ९ ॥

असक्तिरनभिष्वङ्गः पुत्रदारगृहादिषु ।
नित्यं च समचित्तत्वमिष्टानिष्टोपपत्तिषु ॥ १० ॥

1   Arjuna asked:
     What is Prakriti and Purusha, what is the Field and the
        knower of the Field,
     what is knowledge and what is knowable?

2   Krishna replied:
     This body is called the Field,
     the man who masters it is called the Knower of the Field.

3   I am the Knower of all Fields;
     what is knowable is knowledge
        of the Field and its Knower.

4   Listen to me well if you wish to know what the Field is,
        what its qualities are,
     what effects are born of what causes, and also who the
        Knower is and what his attributes are.

5   Variously have sages sung it, in delightful songs,
     in shlokas of clarity and power, for the glory of Brahman.

6   The qualities of the Field are these:
     the elements, egoism, the intellect and the invisible mind,
        the ten senses,

7   Lust, anger, pleasure and pain;
     intelligence, patience; and the sum of all these.

8   Knowledge of the Field consists of the following:
     humility, non-pride, ahimsa, dignity, tranquillity, homage,
        chastity, self-control, and steadfastness;

9   Abandonment of sensual desires, absence of egoism;
     meditation on defects of birth, of age and death, sickness
        and sorrow;

10   Non-attachment even to son, wife and home,
     single-minded faith in me;

मयि चानन्ययोगेन भक्तिरव्यभिचारिणी ।
विविक्तदेशसेवित्वमरतिर्जनसंसदि ॥ ११ ॥

अध्यात्मज्ञाननित्यत्वं तत्त्वज्ञानार्थदर्शनम् ।
एतज्ज्ञानमिति प्रोक्तमज्ञानं यदतोऽन्यथा ॥ १२ ॥

ज्ञेयं यत्तत्प्रवक्ष्यामि यज्ज्ञात्वामृतमश्नुते ।
अनादिमत्परं ब्रह्म न सत्तन्नासदुच्यते ॥ १३ ॥

सर्वतःपाणिपादं तत्सर्वतोऽक्षिशिरोमुखम् ।
सर्वतःश्रुतिमल्लोके सर्वमावृत्य तिष्ठति ॥ १४ ॥

सर्वेन्द्रियगुणाभासं सर्वेन्द्रियविवर्जितम् ।
असक्तं सर्वभृच्चैव निर्गुणं गुणभोक्तृ च ॥ १५ ॥

बहिरन्तश्च भूतानामचरं चरमेव च ।
सूक्ष्मत्वात्तदविज्ञेयं दूरस्थं चान्तिके च तत् ॥ १६ ॥

अविभक्तं च भूतेषु विभक्तमिव च स्थितम् ।
भूतभर्तृ च तज्ज्ञेयं ग्रसिष्णु प्रभविष्णु च ॥ १७ ॥

ज्योतिषामपि तज्ज्योतिस्तमसः परमुच्यते ।
ज्ञानं ज्ञेयं ज्ञानगम्यं हृदि सर्वस्य विष्ठितम् ॥ १८ ॥

इति क्षेत्रं तथा ज्ञानं ज्ञेयं चोक्तं समासतः ।
मद्भक्त एतद्विज्ञाय मद्भावायोपपद्यते ॥ १९ ॥

प्रकृतिं पुरुषं चैव विद्ध्यनादी उभावपि ।
विकारांश्च गुणांश्चैव विद्धि प्रकृतिसम्भवान् ॥ २० ॥

कार्यकरणकर्तृत्वे हेतुः प्रकृतिरुच्यते ।
पुरुषः सुखदुःखानां भोक्तृत्वे हेतुरुच्यते ॥ २१ ॥

पुरुषः प्रकृतिस्थो हि भुङ्क्ते प्रकृतिजान्गुणान् ।
कारणं गुणसङ्गोऽस्य सदसद्योनिजन्मसु ॥ २२ ॥

11   Pilgrimage to places of quiet,
      discontent with crowds;

12   Persistence in spiritual struggle, awareness of the end of
         knowledge.
      The opposite of all this is ignorance.

13   I will tell you what must be known: knowing which,
         immortality is possible.
      What must be known is neither being nor non-being.

14   Its hands, feet and ears are everywhere;
      it stands, straddling the three worlds.

15   It is radiant with the senses, yet not sensual.
      It is despotic, yet it invigorates everything.

16   It is outside and inside life, it is the animate and the inanimate;
      it is ineffable, it is far and near.

17   It is one, yet split up into a myriad beings:
      it is the sustainer of beings, their destroyer and creator.

18   It is the light of lights, shining through darkness:
      it is the only knowledge worth knowing; it is the end of
         knowledge, it exists in everyone's heart.

19   This is the nature of the Field.
      This is the knowledge that must be known.

20   Prakriti and Purusha are without any beginning,
      and all the interplay of the senses is the result of Prakriti.

21   Prakriti is the cause of the body's and the senses' evolution,
      Purusha the cause of the feelings of pleasure and pain.

22   Hidden in Prakriti, Purusha experiences the Prakriti-
         produced senses;
      his birth in pure or impure wombs is the result of this
         attachment.

उपद्रष्टानुमन्ता च भर्ता भोक्ता महेश्वरः ।
परमात्मेति चाप्युक्तो देहेऽस्मिन्पुरुषः परः ॥ २३ ॥

य एवं वेत्ति पुरुषं प्रकृतिं च गुणैः सह ।
सर्वथा वर्तमानोऽपि न स भूयोऽभिजायते ॥ २४ ॥

ध्यानेनात्मनि पश्यन्ति केचिदात्मानमात्मना ।
अन्ये सांख्येन योगेन कर्मयोगेन चापरे ॥ २५ ॥

अन्ये त्वेवमजानन्तः श्रुत्वान्येभ्य उपासते ।
तेऽपि चातितरन्त्येव मृत्युं श्रुतिपरायणाः ॥ २६ ॥

यावत्संजायते किंचित्सत्त्वं स्थावरजङ्गमम् ।
क्षेत्रक्षेत्रज्ञसंयोगात्तद्विद्धि भरतर्षभ ॥ २७ ॥

समं सर्वेषु भूतेषु तिष्ठन्तं परमेश्वरम् ।
विनश्यत्स्वविनश्यन्तं यः पश्यति स पश्यति ॥ २८ ॥

समं पश्यन्हि सर्वत्र समवस्थितमीश्वरम् ।
न हिनस्त्यात्मनात्मानं ततो याति परां गतिम् ॥ २९ ॥

प्रकृत्यैव च कर्माणि क्रियमाणानि सर्वशः ।
यः पश्यति तथात्मानमकर्तारं स पश्यति ॥ ३० ॥

यदा भूतपृथग्भावमेकस्थमनुपश्यति ।
तत एव च विस्तारं ब्रह्म सम्पद्यते तदा ॥ ३१ ॥

अनादित्वान्निर्गुणत्वात्परमात्मायमव्ययः ।
शरीरस्थोऽपि कौन्तेय न करोति न लिप्यते ॥ ३२ ॥

यथा सर्वगतं सौक्ष्म्यादाकाशं नोपलिप्यते ।
सर्वत्रावस्थितो देहे तथात्मा नोपलिप्यते ॥ ३३ ॥

23 The supreme Purusha is also the Witness,
the Permitter, the Sustainer and the Enjoyer, the highest
God, the Supreme Soul.

24 The man who understands Purusha and Prakriti
exhausts his succession of births.

25 Some through devotion see the atman;
others choose the path of knowledge;
still others follow the path of action.

26 Others, unaware of this, worship by hearsay;
these also are saved, for they have faith.

27 Whatever creature is born, animate or inanimate,
is born of the union between the Field and the Knower.

28 His vision is clear who sees Brahman as equal in all beings,
as the non-material in the material.

29 And seeing Brahman equal in all beings,
he takes care not to injure Brahman by the atman,
and achieves the supreme goal.

30 His vision is clear, too,
who sees all actions as the work of Prakriti, and the atman
as unaffected.

31 And when he sees in the scattered existences of all beings
an essential unity,
he becomes Brahman.

32 Beginningless and feelingless,
this unchangeable atman neither acts nor is affected by acts,
though it is lodged in the body.

33 As the all-embracing sky is pure though it spreads
everywhere,
so the atman, everywhere scattered, remains always pure.

यथा प्रकाशयत्येकः कृत्स्नं लोकमिमं रविः ।
क्षेत्रं क्षेत्री तथा कृत्स्नं प्रकाशयति भारत॥ ३४ ॥

क्षेत्रक्षेत्रज्ञयोरेवमन्तरं ज्ञानचक्षुषा ।
भूतप्रकृतिमोक्षं च ये विदुर्यान्ति ते परम् ॥ ३५ ॥

34 As a single sun illuminates this vast earth,
    so he who lives in the Field illuminates the entire Field.

35 And those who can distinguish clearly
    between the Field and the Knower
        eventually reach the supreme goal.

THE DIFFERENT GUNAS

*I*f Purusha is the 'light of lights', what is Prakriti? Prakriti, explains Krishna, is 'my womb, and I place the seed in it'. Prakriti is primordial matter, both crude and subtle. It consists of three gunas or qualities (literally, 'thread'). The three threads that, in varying permutations and combinations, make up all material phenomena are: sattva, rajas, tamas. These have been translated and interpreted in all manner of ways. Very simply, sattva is the quality of light, goodness, knowledge, vitality; rajas the quality of grayness, amorality, curiosity, physical strength; tamas the quality of darkness, immorality, ignorance, laziness. The permutations and combinations of these gunas are endless, and each person is dominated, at different times, by one or the other of these gunas, which provide the unique stamp of individuality, of character, of personality. But this personality is Prakriti-based; it is grounded in a mix of raw and refined tendencies, inclinations, proclivities, behaviour patterns. They are not the real person, the Purusha. The aim of life is to see through and overcome these physical guna-pulls and arrive at a clear awareness of one's real Self.

The key last but one shloka of Canto XIV makes this an unequivocal requirement of the spiritual aspirant: 'My unswerving devotee transcends the gunas and is ready for union with Brahman.'

श्रीभगवानुवाच

परं भूयः प्रवक्ष्यामि ज्ञानानां ज्ञानमुत्तमम् ।
यज्ज्ञात्वा मुनयः सर्वे परां सिद्धिमितो गताः ॥ १ ॥

इदं ज्ञानमुपाश्रित्य मम साधर्म्यमागताः ।
सर्गेऽपि नोपजायन्ते प्रलये न व्यथन्ति च ॥ २ ॥

मम योनिर्महद्ब्रह्म तस्मिन्गर्भं दधाम्यहम् ।
संभवः सर्वभूतानां ततो भवति भारत ॥ ३ ॥

सर्वयोनिषु कौन्तेय मूर्तयः सम्भवन्ति याः ।
तासां ब्रह्म महद्योनिरहं बीजप्रदः पिता ॥ ४ ॥

सत्त्वं रजस्तम इति गुणाः प्रकृतिसंभवाः ।
निबध्नन्ति महाबाहो देहे देहिनमव्ययम् ॥ ५ ॥

तत्र सत्त्वं निर्मलत्वात्प्रकाशकमनामयम् ।
सुखसङ्गेन बध्नाति ज्ञानसङ्गेन चानघ ॥ ६ ॥

रजो रागात्मकं विद्धि तृष्णासङ्गसमुद्भवम् ।
तन्निबध्नाति कौन्तेय कर्मसङ्गेन देहिनम् ॥ ७ ॥

तमस्त्वज्ञानजं विद्धि मोहनं सर्वदेहिनाम् ।
प्रमादालस्यनिद्राभिस्तन्निबध्नाति भारत ॥ ८ ॥

सत्त्वं सुखे सञ्जयति रजः कर्मणि भारत ।
ज्ञानमावृत्य तु तमः प्रमादे सञ्जयत्युत ॥ ९ ॥

रजस्तमश्चाभिभूय सत्त्वं भवति भारत ।
रजः सत्त्वं तमश्चैव तमः सत्त्वं रजस्तथा ॥ १० ॥

सर्वद्वारेषु देहेऽस्मिन्प्रकाश उपजायते ।
ज्ञानं यदा तदा विद्याद्विवृद्धं सत्त्वमित्युत ॥ ११ ॥

लोभः प्रवृत्तिरारम्भः कर्मणामशमः स्पृहा ।
रजस्येतानि जायन्ते विवृद्धे भरतर्षभ ॥ १२ ॥

अप्रकाशोऽप्रवृत्तिश्च प्रमादो मोह एव च ।
तमस्येतानि जायन्ते विवृद्धे कुरूनन्दन ॥ १३ ॥

1   Krishna said:
     I will now give you the greatest knowledge of all,
     through which the sages have achieved perfection.

2   They are not subject to rebirth at the time of creation,
     nor are they affected at the time of the world's dissolution.

3   The great Prakriti is my womb, and I place the seed in it;
     in this way, Arjuna, life begins.

4   Remember: whatever form of birth there is in this world,
     the great Prakriti is the ultimate womb, and I am the seed-
          giving father.

5   Sattva, rajas and tamas —
     these Prakriti-produced gunas unite the body to the atman.

6   Sattva unites with purity and luminosity;
     its points of reference are happiness and knowledge.

7   Rajas is the quality of passion, it causes unrest and attachment;
     it unites by creating attachment to action.

8   Tamas is born of ignorance:
     it unites through unknowing, torpor and sleep.

9   Sattva refers to happiness, rajas to action;
     tamas, stifling discrimination, to unknowing,

10   Sattva occasionally rules over rajas and tamas;
     rajas over sattva and tamas, and tamas over sattva and rajas.

11   When the light of wisdom penetrates every sense,
     sattva is predominant.

12   Cupidity and desire to work, restlessness and passion
     are born when rajas rules.

13   Darkness, sloth, misunderstanding and delusion
     are born when tamas rules.

यदा सत्त्वे प्रवृद्धे तु प्रलयं याति देहभृत् ।
तदोत्तमविदां लोकानमलान्प्रतिपद्यते ॥ १४ ॥

रजसि प्रलयं गत्वा कर्मसङ्गिषु जायते ।
तथा प्रलीनस्तमसि मूढयोनिषु जायते ॥ १५ ॥

कर्मणः सुकृतस्याहुः सात्त्विकं निर्मलं फलम् ।
रजसस्तु फलं दुःखमज्ञानं तमसः फलम् ॥ १६ ॥

सत्त्वात्संचायते ज्ञानं रजसो लोभ एव च ।
प्रमादमोहौ तमसो भवतोऽज्ञानमेव च ॥ १७ ॥

ऊर्ध्वं गच्छन्ति सत्त्वस्था मध्ये तिष्ठन्ति राजसाः ।
जघन्यगुणवृत्तिस्था अधो गच्छन्ति तामसाः ॥ १८ ॥

नान्यं गुणेभ्यः कर्तारं यदा द्रष्टानुपश्यति ।
गुणेभ्यश्च परं वेत्ति मद्भावं सोऽधिगच्छति ॥ १९ ॥

गुणानेतानतीत्य त्रीन्देही देहसमुद्भवान् ।
जन्ममृत्युजरादुःखैर्विमुक्तोऽमृतमश्नुते ॥ २० ॥

अर्जुन उवाच
कैर्लिङ्गैस्त्रीन्गुणानेतानतीतो भवति प्रभो ।
किमाचारः कथं चैतांस्त्रीन्गुणानतिवर्तते ॥ २१ ॥

श्रीभगवानुवाच
प्रकाशं च प्रवृत्तिं च मोहमेव च पाण्डव ।
न द्वेष्टि संप्रवृत्तानि न निवृत्तानि काङ्क्षति ॥ २२ ॥

उदासीनवदासीनो गुणैर्यो न विचाल्यते ।
गुणा वर्तन्त इत्येव योऽवतिष्ठति नेङ्गते ॥ २३ ॥

समदुःखसुखः स्वस्थः समलोष्टाश्मकाञ्चनः ।
तुल्यप्रियाप्रियो धीरस्तुल्यनिन्दात्मसंस्तुतिः ॥ २४ ॥

14   And if the atman meet death during
         sattva's predominance,
     it straightaway reaches the pure regions of the knowers of
         wisdom.

15   Death in rajas means birth among the action-obsessed;
     death in tamas means birth among the unreasoning.

16   The fruits of noble action are sattva and gentle;
     the fruits of rajas agony, of tamas ignorance.

17   Wisdom is the result of sattva, and lust of rajas;
     ignorance, misunderstanding and delusion of tamas.

18   The sattvika go up, the rajasika hang in midspace,
     the tamasika, caught in the lowest guna, go down.

19   When the sage sees no other worker but the gunas
     and sees also what is beyond the gunas, he reaches me.

20   The atman which transcends matter-involved gunas is
         untouched by birth and death,
     decay and sorrow, and finds immortality.

21   Arjuna asked:
     How does one recognize the transcender of the gunas?
     how does he behave, what does he do with his life?

22   Krishna replied:
     He does not dislike light, he does not dislike work,
     he does not desire them when he is without them;

23   He behaves detachedly;
     he knows the gunas are working,
         and he remains steady;

24   He remains serene in pain and joy, or when considering a
         piece of earth, a stone or a lump of gold;
     he remains serene in moments of glory and shame;

मानापमानयोस्तुल्यस्तुल्यो मित्रारिपक्षयोः ।
सर्वारम्भपरित्यागी गुणातीतः स उच्यते ॥ २५ ॥

मां च योऽव्यभिचारेण भक्तियोगेन सेवते ।
स गुणान्समतीत्यैतान्ब्रह्मभूयाय कल्पते ॥ २६ ॥

ब्रह्मणो हि प्रतिष्ठाहममृतस्याव्ययस्य च ।
शाश्वतस्य च धर्मस्य सुखस्यैकान्तिकस्य च ॥ २७ ॥

25   He remains serene in honour and dishonour; he has
       abandoned worldly undertakings.
     Such a man is said to have transcended the gunas.

26   My unswerving devotee
     transcends the gunas and is ready for union with Brahman.

27   For I am the abode of Brahman, the deathless and the
       unchanging,
     the abode of eternal dharma and supreme felicity.

THE HIGHEST PURUSHA

*F*rom *Prakriti to Purusha —
in fact, as the title of Canto XV says, to 'Purushottama', the 'Highest
Purusha'.*

*One of Hinduism's most beautiful, memorable and meaningful
religious symbols is presented in the four opening shlokas of this Canto.
It is the symbol of the Kalpa-Taru, the Imagination Tree or the Wish-
Fulfilling Tree.*

*Why does Krishna introduce the cosmic fig-tree Ashvattha with
roots above, shoots mid-space, and fruits below? 'Cut down this tree,
Arjuna,' he says, 'with the sword of detachment. And stand up!' The
suggestion, of course, is that the network of ruthless Karma, produced by
Prakriti, embraces sky, earth, and underworld; affects gods, men, and
anti-gods (as Prajapati explains in the Brihadaranyaka Upanishad);
involves pre-life, this life, and after-life (Kala in Sanskrit is Time for
yesterday, today and tomorrow).*

*But there is another triad presented in this Canto which is of
profound significance: the Purusha Trinity. One Purusha is embedded
in the body — embodied. This is the perishable Spirit. The second Purusha
is the imperishable atman which enters the body but leaves it, taking
with it the subtle impressions of the senses, like a breeze carrying the
fragrance of flowers. But there is a third, the Paramatma Purusha, the
'deathless Lord', who is honoured in the key shloka 18 of Canto XV: 'I
am above the perishable and the imperishable; therefore, the world and
the Vedas call me the Highest Purusha, Purushottama.' When the tree
of Karma is sliced with non-attachment, Purushottama is attained.*

श्रीभगवानुवाच

ऊर्ध्वमूलमधःशाखमश्वत्थं प्राहुरव्ययम् ।
छन्दांसि यस्य पर्णानि यस्तं वेद स वेदवित् ॥ १ ॥

अधश्चोर्ध्वं प्रसृतास्तस्य शाखा
         गुणप्रवृद्धा विषयप्रवालाः ।
अधश्च मूलान्यनुसंततानि
         कर्मानुबन्धीनि मनुष्यलोके ॥ २ ॥

न रूपमस्येह तथोपलभ्यते
         नान्तो न चादिर्न च संप्रतिष्ठा ।
अश्वत्थमेनं सुविरूढमूल-
         मसङ्गशस्त्रेण दृढेन छित्त्वा ॥ ३ ॥

ततः पदं तत्परिमार्गितव्यं यस्मिन्गता न निवर्तन्ति भूयः ।
तमेव चाद्यं पुरुषं प्रपद्ये यतः प्रवृत्तिः प्रसृता पुराणी ॥ ४ ॥

निर्मानमोहा जितसङ्गदोषा
         अध्यात्मनित्या विनिवृत्तकामाः ।
द्वन्द्वैर्विमुक्ताः सुखदुःखसंज्ञै-
         र्गच्छन्त्यमूढाः पदमव्ययं तत् ॥ ५ ॥

न तद्भासयते सूर्यो न शशाङ्को न पावकः ।
यद्गत्वा न निवर्तन्ते तद्धाम परमं मम ॥ ६ ॥

ममैवांशो जीवलोके जीवभूतः सनातनः ।
मनःषष्ठानीन्द्रियाणि प्रकृतिस्थानि कर्षति ॥ ७ ॥

शरीरं यदवाप्नोति यच्चाप्युत्क्रामतीश्वरः ।
गृहीत्वैतानि संयाति वायुर्गन्धानिवाशयात् ॥ ८ ॥

श्रोत्रं चक्षुः स्पर्शनं च रसनं घ्राणमेव च ।
अधिष्ठाय मनश्चायं विषयानुपसेवते ॥ ९ ॥

उत्क्रामन्तं स्थितं वापि भुञ्जानं वा गुणान्वितम् ।
विमूढा नानुपश्यन्ति पश्यन्ति ज्ञानचक्षुषः ॥ १० ॥

1   Krishna continued:
Mention is made of a cosmic fig-tree rooted above,
    whose leaves are said to be the Vedas;
the knower of this fig-tree is the knower of the Vedas.

2   Its branches reach out below and above, and the gunas
    nourish them;
its flowers are the objects of the senses; below the ground
    flourish more roots, giving birth to action.

3   You may not see its real shape, nor its end, birth and existence.
Slice this fig-tree with non-attachment!

4   And hope for the end of karma, saying:
I shelter in the Purusha that causes
    the birth of the eternal cycle.

5   Free from vanity, delusion, and attachment, passions under
    control,
and unmoved by opposites, the clear-thinking man finds
    the supreme goal.

6   The sun does not illuminate this goal, nor the moon, nor fire;
this goal is my abode, and to achieve it means the end of
    karma.

7   An eternal fragment of myself becomes an atman in the
    worldly cycle,
and pulls the Prakriti-bound mind and senses of itself.

8   So Brahman enters a body or discards it,
like a breeze receiving the fragrance of flowers.

9   Supervising the ear, the eye, touch, taste and smell,
and also the mind, he enjoys the objects of the senses.

10   The foolish do not see him transmigrating,
or living in the gunas or enjoying them, but the wise do.

यतन्तो योगिनश्चैनं पश्यन्त्यात्मन्यवस्थितम् ।
यतन्तोऽप्यकृतात्मानो नैनं पश्यन्त्यचेतसः ॥ ११ ॥

यदादित्यगतं तेजो जगद्भासयतेऽखिलम् ।
यच्चन्द्रमसि यच्चाग्नौ तत्तेजो विद्धि मामकम् ॥ १२ ॥

गामाविश्य च भूतानि धारयाम्यहमोजसा ।
पुष्णामि चौषधीः सर्वाः सोमो भूत्वा रसात्मकः ॥ १३ ॥

अहं वैश्वानरो भूत्वा प्राणिनां देहमाश्रितः ।
प्राणापानसमायुक्तः पचाम्यन्नं चतुर्विधम् ॥ १४ ॥

सर्वस्य चाहं हृदि संनिविष्टो
मत्तः स्मृतिर्ज्ञानमपोहनं च ।
वेदैश्च सर्वैरहमेव वेद्यो
वेदान्तकृद्वेदविदेव चाहम् ॥ १५ ॥

द्वाविमौ पुरुषौ लोके क्षरश्चाक्षर एव च ।
क्षरः सर्वाणि भूतानि कूटस्थोऽक्षर उच्यते ॥ १६ ॥

उत्तमः पुरुषस्त्वन्यः परमात्मेत्युदाहृतः ।
यो लोकत्रयमाविश्य बिभर्त्यव्यय ईश्वरः ॥ १७ ॥

यस्मात्क्षरमतीतोऽहमक्षरादपि चोत्तमः ।
अतोऽस्मि लोके वेदे च प्रथितः पुरुषोत्तमः ॥ १८ ॥

यो मामेवमसम्मूढो जानाति पुरुषोत्तमम् ।
स सर्वविद्भजति मां सर्वभावेन भारत ॥ १९ ॥

इति गुह्यतमं शास्त्रमिदमुक्तं मयानघ ।
एतद्बुद्ध्वा बुद्धिमान्स्यात्कृतकृत्यश्च भारत ॥ २० ॥

11 Struggling yogis see him in themselves, but the less subtle
     and wise,
    in spite of their devotion, fail to do so.

12 The light living in the sun which illumines the world,
    the light in the moon and in fire, are mine.

13 Nourishing the earth with energy, I sustain life;
    becoming the fluid moon, I feed plants.

14 And living in life as the vital fire,
    I digest the four kinds of food.

15 I live in all hearts; memory and feeling, lack of memory and
     lack of feeling proceed from me;
    I am what the Vedas want to know, I am knowledge of the
     Vedas, and the knower of the Vedas.

16 Two kinds of Purushas exist in the world —the perishable
     and the imperishable:
    bodies are the perishable, the Self is the imperishable.

17 Another, the Supreme Purusha, is the Highest Soul,
    the deathless Lord, whose energy sustains the three worlds.

18 I am above the perishable and the imperishable;
    therefore the world and the Vedas call me the Highest
     Purusha — Purushottama.

19 The man who sees me as the Highest Purusha, Purushottama,
    is the man who adores me with his whole heart.

20 I give you this profound teaching
    in the hope that you will reach supreme wisdom.

DIVINE AND ANTI-DIVINE NATURES

*T*he Hindu hell is temporary, *of course, and very easy to enter. According to the key last shloka of Canto XVI, 'Hell has three gates — lust, anger, and greed (kama, krodha, lobha).' For the sake of his atman, Arjuna is advised to give up all three.*

After the magnificent epiphany of the Wishing Tree symbol, the sermonizing of Canto XVI may seem a bit of an anti-climax. There is, however, a practical reason for the long, meticulous detailing of the divine nature and the anti-divine nature. Arjuna must have started wondering if there is for him any hope at all of attaining the Highest Purusha. The high-flying ethical idealism and luxuriant symbology might appear to be outside the ken of a Kshatriya.

Not so, suggests Krishna. The caste system, to which Krishna has referred earlier, is well and fine — and not so well and fine. The three gunas are useful aids to plumb the nature of human behaviour — and not so useful aids. The three Purushas are splendid philosophical constructs — and not so splendid too.

What really matters is whether a person is well meaning or not. This is the ultimate, and only significant, distinction. Am I deva or asura, divine or anti-divine? Am I seriously motivated, constructively inclined; or am I aggressive, flippant, negative? It is not difficult to find that out, because that classification cuts across guna, caste, creed, and race. So, Krishna's message of goodwill and hope: 'Divine birth leads to moksha, anti-divine to bondage. Do not worry, Arjuna, your birth is divine.'

श्रीभगवानुवाच

अभयं सत्त्वसंशुद्धिर्ज्ञानयोगव्यवस्थितिः ।
दानं दमश्च यज्ञश्च स्वाध्यायस्तप आर्जवम् ॥ १ ॥

अहिंसा सत्यमक्रोधस्त्यागः शान्तिरपैशुनम् ।
दया भूतेष्वलोलुप्त्वं मार्दवं ह्रीरचापलम् ॥ २ ॥

तेजः क्षमा धृतिः शौचमद्रोहो नातिमानिता ।
भवन्ति सम्पदं दैवीमभिजातस्य भारत ॥ ३ ॥

दम्भो दर्पोऽभिमानश्च क्रोधः पारुष्यमेव च ।
अज्ञानं चाभिजातस्य पार्थ सम्पदमासुरीम् ॥ ४ ॥

दैवी सम्पद्विमोक्षाय निबन्धायासुरी मता ।
मा शुचः सम्पदं दैवीमभिजातोऽसि पाण्डव ॥ ५ ॥

द्वौ भूतसर्गौ लोकेऽस्मिन्दैव आसुर एव च ।
दैवो विस्तरशः प्रोक्त आसुरं पार्थ मे शृणु ॥ ६ ॥

प्रवृत्तिं च निवृत्तिं च जना न विदुरासुराः ।
न शौचं नापि चाचारो न सत्यं तेषु विद्यते ॥ ७ ॥

असत्यमप्रतिष्ठं ते जगदाहुरनीश्वरम् ।
अपरस्परसम्भूतं किमन्यत्कामहैतुकम् ॥ ८ ॥

एतां दृष्टिमवष्टभ्य नष्टात्मानोऽल्पबुद्धयः ।
प्रभवन्त्युग्रकर्माणः क्षयाय जगतोऽहिताः ॥ ९ ॥

काममाश्रित्य दुष्पूरं दम्भमानमदान्विताः ।
मोहाद्गृहीत्वासद्ग्राहान्प्रवर्तन्तेऽशुचिव्रताः ॥ १० ॥

चिन्तामपरिमेयां च प्रलयान्तामुपाश्रिताः ।
कामोपभोगपरमा एतावदिति निश्चिताः ॥ ११ ॥

1   Krishna continued:
      Absence of fear, a pure heart, firmness in the path of
         knowledge;
      charity, persistence, sacrifice, and study of scriptures;

2   Simplicity, integrity, non-violence, truth, mercy, modesty,
         kindness;
      absence of desires that lead to frustration;

3   Courage, compassion, patience, purity —
      these are signs of the divine nature.

4   Pride, obstreperousness, vanity, anger,
      boorishness and ignorance are marks of the anti-divine nature.

5   Divine birth leads to moksha, and anti-divine to bondage.
      Do not fear, Arjuna, your birth is divine.

6   Two kinds of people inhabit this earth —the divine and the
         anti-divine; the divine I have explained to you;
      let me explain the anti-divine.

7   The anti-divine confuse what should be done with what
         should not be done:
      they have neither virtue, nor good conduct, not truth.

8   They say:
      The world is false and immoral, godless, and born of lust.

9   With these beliefs, these unfortunate people
      become the world's enemies and its potential destroyers.

10   Hypocritical, vain and fierce, inflated with overreaching
         ambition, they let their ignorance breed ill thoughts,
      and strive for the world's ruin.

11   Tormented by endless worries which only death ends,
      considering sensual pleasure as the only goal in this world,

आशापाशशतैर्बद्धाः कामक्रोधपरायणाः ।
ईहन्ते कामभोगार्थमन्यायेनार्थसञ्चयान् ॥ १२ ॥

इदमद्य मया लब्धमिमं प्राप्स्ये मनोरथम् ।
इदमस्तीदमपि मे भविष्यति पुनर्धनम् ॥ १३ ॥

असौ मया हतः शत्रुर्हनिष्ये चापरानपि ।
ईश्वरोऽहमहं भोगी सिद्धोऽहं बलवान्सुखी ॥ १४ ॥

आढ्योऽभिजनवानस्मि कोऽन्योऽस्ति सदृशो मया ।
यक्ष्ये दास्यामि मोदिष्य इत्यज्ञानविमोहिताः ॥ १५ ॥

अनेकचित्तविभ्रान्ता मोहजालसमावृताः ।
प्रसक्ताः कामभोगेषु पतन्ति नरकेऽशुचौ ॥ १६ ॥

आत्मसम्भाविताः स्तब्धा धनमानमदान्विताः ।
यजन्ते नामयज्ञैस्ते दम्भेनाविधिपूर्वकम् ॥ १७ ॥

अहङ्कारं बलं दर्पं कामं क्रोधं च संश्रिताः ।
मामात्मपरदेहेषु प्रद्विषन्तोऽभ्यसूयकाः ॥ १८ ॥

तानहं द्विषतः क्रूरान्संसारेषु नराधमान् ।
क्षिपाम्यजस्रमशुभानासुरीष्वेव योनिषु ॥ १९ ॥

आसुरीं योनिमापन्ना मूढा जन्मनि जन्मनि ।
मामप्राप्यैव कौन्तेय ततो यान्त्यधमां गतिम् ॥ २० ॥

त्रिविधं नरकस्येदं द्वारं नाशनमात्मनः ।
कामः क्रोधस्तथा लोभस्तस्मादेतत्त्रयं त्यजेत् ॥ २१ ॥

एतैर्विमुक्तः कौन्तेय तमोद्वारैस्त्रिभिर्नरः ।
आचरत्यात्मनः श्रेयस्ततो याति परां गतिम् ॥ २२ ॥

12   Locked in their lust, ambition, and anger,
      they run after sensual delights.

13   'Today I enjoyed this, tomorrow I'll enjoy that;
      this I have, that I'll get tomorrow;

14   'I killed this enemy today,
          tomorrow I'll get rid of others.
      I am king; I enjoy.'

15   'I know success, power and pleasure. I have untold wealth,
          I was born auspicious. Who is like me?'
      Deluding themselves,

16   Whirled in their own bewilderment,
          slaves of the ego,
      they fall into a horrible hell.

17   Vain, selfish, and obsessed with possessions,
      they pay lip service to dharma;

18   Insolent and passionate,
      they loathe the atman in themselves and in others.

19   I cast these foolish ill-doers
      always in the wombs of the anti-divine.

20   Born from anti-divine wombs,
          ignorant from their birth,
      they fail to reach me,
          and become even worse in their next birth.

21   Hell has three gates —lust, anger, and greed.
      For your own sake, Arjuna, give up these three.

22   If a man gives up these three, and is absorbed in his own
          improvement,
      he may find the supreme goal.

य: शास्त्रविधिमुत्सृज्य वर्तते कामकारत: ।
न स सिद्धिमवाप्नोति न सुखं न परां गतिम् ॥ २३ ॥

तस्माच्छास्त्रं प्रमाणं ते कार्याकार्यव्यवस्थितौ ।
ज्ञात्वा शास्त्रविधानोक्तं कर्म कर्तुमिहार्हसि ॥ २४ ॥

23   But the man who ignores the rules of the scriptures, and
         is moved to action by impulse and lust,
         never finds perfection;
     no happiness for him, no supreme goal.

24   The scriptures tell you what should be done and what
         avoided:
     your actions should conform to the truths of the scriptures.

THE THREE DEVOTIONS

*C*anto XVII is all about shraddha, which I have here translated as 'devotion' instead of 'faith', because earlier Krishna has described how faith blossoms into devotion. If, as Krishna informs Arjuna, 'your birth is divine', it follows that Arjuna's heart is in the right place, his faith is well-meaning, his moksha is assured. But is it really?

A man is what his faith is (yat shraddhah sa eva sah). But a man may be sattvika, rajasika, or tamasika. The sattvika man's faith leads him to worship gods, the rajasika worships rakshasas, the tamsika spirits and ghosts. Is faith enough?

No, says Krishna. More important is the Truth That Is (Om Tat Sat). Shloka 23 adds that everything —Brahmins, Vedas, rituals — proceeds from the Truth That Is. What is this Truth That Is? Om, we know, is the all-embracing sacred syllable, and requires all manner of complex, even mystic gloss; Tat is that, which is mysteriously vague; and Sat is Is, 'Isness', but 'isness' has an inscape not easy to put one's finger on.

Shraddha requires something more than abstractions. Chant Om Tat Sat, by all means, advises Krishna. Faith is fine, and Om Tat Sat are fine, but put feeling in the faith and the chanting. Too many devotees perform mechanical, ritual, push-button shraddha. Such shraddha is 'asat', unreal, valueless. Hence the key last shloka: 'Unreal is giving without feeling, action without feeling, discipline without feeling. Useless in this world and the next.'

अर्जुन उवाच

ये शास्त्रविधिमुत्सृज्य यजन्ते श्रद्धयान्विताः ।
तेषां निष्ठा तु का कृष्ण सत्त्वमाहो रजस्तमः ॥ १ ॥

श्रीभगवानुवाच

त्रिविधा भवति श्रद्धा देहिनां सा स्वभावजा ।
सात्त्विका राजसी चैव तामसी चेति तां शृणु ॥ २ ॥

सत्त्वानुरूपा सर्वस्य श्रद्धा भवति भारत ।
श्रद्धामयोऽयं पुरुषो यो यच्छ्रद्धः स एव सः ॥ ३ ॥

यजन्ते सात्त्विका देवान्यक्षरक्षांसि राजसाः ।
प्रेतान्भूतगणांश्चान्ये यजन्ते तामसा जनाः ॥ ४ ॥

अशास्त्रविहितं घोरं तप्यन्ते ये तपो जनाः ।
दम्भाहंकारसंयुक्ताः कामरागबलान्विताः ॥ ५ ॥

कर्शयन्तः शरीरस्थं भूतग्राममचेतसः ।
मां चैवान्तःशरीरस्थं तान्विद्ध्यासुरनिश्चयान् ॥ ६ ॥

आहारस्त्वपि सर्वस्य त्रिविधो भवति प्रियः ।
यज्ञस्तपस्तथा दानं तेषां भेदमिमं शृणु ॥ ७ ॥

आयुःसत्त्वबलारोग्यसुखप्रीतिविवर्धनाः ।
रस्याः स्निग्धाः स्थिरा हृद्या आहाराः सात्त्विकप्रियाः ॥ ८ ॥

कट्वम्ललवणात्युष्णतीक्ष्णरूक्षविदाहिनः ।
आहारा राजसस्येष्टा दुःखशोकामयप्रदाः ॥ ९ ॥

यातयामं गतरसं पूति पर्युषितं च यत् ।
उच्छिष्टमपि चामेध्यं भोजनं तामसप्रियम् ॥ १० ॥

अफलाकाङ्क्षिभिर्यज्ञो विधिदृष्टो य इज्यते ।
यष्टव्यमेवेति मनः समाधाय स सात्त्विकः ॥ ११ ॥

1   Arjuna asked:
     What is the condition of those who set aside the scriptures
        but perform their duties with devotion?
     Is it sattvika, rajasika, or tamasika?

2   Krishna replied:
     Let me tell you what it is.
     The atman knows three types of devotion: sattvika, rajasika,
        tamasika.

3   Each person's nature dictates his manner of devotion:
     a man is what his faith is.

4   For which reason, sattvika men worship the gods,
     the rajasika worship the rakshasas,
        the tamasika spirits and ghosts.

5   And anti-gods are worshipped
     by unthinking men,

6   Who torture the atman with lust and selfishness,
     and reject the disciplines laid down in the scriptures.

7   Food, ritual, tapasya, charity —all are different with
        different people.
     Let me explain this to you.

8   The sattvika likes food to be pleasing,
     savoury, juicy, and sustaining.

9   The rajasika likes food to be bitter, sour, salty, dry, burning;
     food that produces pain, sorrow, and ill-health.

10   The tamasika likes left-over and half-cooked food,
     stale, smelly, defiled, and tasteless.

11   Ritual which is sattvika is work performed selflessly,
     satisfying for its own sake, not for reward.

अभिसंधाय तु फलं दम्भार्थमपि चैव यत् ।
इज्यते भरतश्रेष्ठ तं यज्ञं विद्धि राजसम् ॥ १२ ॥

विधिहीनमसृष्टान्नं मन्त्रहीनमदक्षिणम् ।
श्रद्धाविरहितं यज्ञं तामसं परिचक्षते ॥ १३ ॥

देवद्विजगुरुप्राज्ञपूजनं शौचमार्जवम् ।
ब्रह्मचर्यमहिंसा च शारीरं तप उच्यते ॥ १४ ॥

अनुद्वेगकरं वाक्यं सत्यं प्रियहितं च यत् ।
स्वाध्यायाभ्यसनं चैव वाङ्मयं तप उच्यते ॥ १५ ॥

मनःप्रसादः सौम्यत्वं मौनमात्मविनिग्रहः ।
भावसंशुद्धिरित्येतत्तपो मानसमुच्यते ॥ १६ ॥

श्रद्धया परया तप्तं तपस्तत्त्रिविधं नरैः ।
अफलाकाङ्क्षिभिर्युक्तैः सात्त्विकं परिचक्षते ॥ १७ ॥

सत्कारमानपूजार्थं तपो दम्भेन चैव यत् ।
क्रियते तदिह प्रोक्तं राजसं चलमध्रुवम् ॥ १८ ॥

मूढग्राहेणात्मनो यत्पीडया क्रियते तपः ।
परस्योत्सादनार्थं वा तत्तामसमुदाहृतम् ॥ १९ ॥

दातव्यमिति यद्दानं दीयतेऽनुपकारिणे ।
देशे काले च पात्रे च तद्दानं सात्त्विकं स्मृतम् ॥ २० ॥

यत्तु प्रत्युपकारार्थं फलमुद्दिश्य वा पुनः ।
दीयते च परिक्लिष्टं तद्दानं राजसं स्मृतम् ॥ २१ ॥

अदेशकाले यद्दानमपात्रेभ्यश्च दीयते ।
असत्कृतमवज्ञातं तत्तामसमुदाहृतम् ॥ २२ ॥

ॐ तत्सदिति निर्देशो ब्रह्मणस्त्रिविधः स्मृतः ।
ब्राह्मणास्तेन वेदाश्च यज्ञाश्च विहिताः पुरा ॥ २३ ॥

12 Ritual which is rajasika is work for reward,
    performed for the sake of fame and success.

13 Ritual which is tamasika is without mantra,
    without shraddha, without any kind of dedication,
        work that goes against moral principles.

14 Tapasya of the body means respecting gods, Brahmins,
        elders and wise men;
    it involves wisdom and purity, brahmacharya and ahimsa.

15 Tapasya of speech means speaking the truth;
    it involves pleasant and helpful words, and study of the Vedas.

16 Tapasya of the mind means serenity;
    it involves silence, self-control, compassion and honesty,

17 These are the three aspects of sattvika.
    They are practised by men who have devotion.

18 Tapasya used for reward, honour or fame,
    is rajasika —it is transient and treacherous.

19 Tapasya practised for self-torture,
    from folly or malice, is tamasika.

20 Sattvika charity is giving for the sake of giving,
    giving that expects no return, giving at the right time to
        the right person.

21 Rajasika charity is reluctant giving,
    giving that expects return, giving that looks for reward.

22 Tamasika charity is giving to the wrong person at the
        wrong time,
    giving without concern, giving with contempt.

23 Brahman is Om Tat Sat, the Truth That Is;
    Brahmins, Vedas and rituals proceed from the Truth That Is.

तस्मादोमित्युदाहृत्य यज्ञदानतप:क्रिया: ।
प्रवर्तन्ते विधानोक्ता: सततं ब्रह्मवादिनाम् ॥ २४ ॥

तदित्यनभिसंधाय फलं यज्ञतप:क्रिया: ।
दानक्रियाश्च विविधा: क्रियन्ते मोक्षकाङ्क्षिभि: ॥ २५ ॥

सद्भावे साधुभावे च सदित्येतत्प्रयुज्यते ।
प्रशस्ते कर्मणि तथा सच्छब्द: पार्थ युज्यते ॥ २६ ॥

यज्ञे तपसि दाने च स्थिति: सदिति चोच्यते ।
कर्म चैव तदर्थीयं सदित्येवाभिधीयते ॥ २७ ॥

अश्रद्धया हुतं दत्तं तपस्तप्तं कृतं च यत् ।
असदित्युच्यते पार्थ न च तत्प्रेत्य नो इह ॥ २८ ॥

24   Chant Om, when you give charity,
      when you practise discipline, when you perform ritual.

25   Chant Tat,
      and forget the fruits.

26   Chant Sat,
      the Truth and the Good.

27   Firmness in discipline and charity is Sat.
      And action thus performed is Sat; it is real.

28   Unreal is giving without feeling, action without feeling,
         discipline without feeling.
      Useless in this world and in the next.

THE WAY OF SALVATION

$\mathcal{Y}$es, the Gita *is a gospel off action. Krishna exhorts Arjuna to fight, to do his duty, to be a karma-yogi. But it is also a gospel of knowledge. No action is complete, or desirable, without knowing why, how and when to act. So Arjuna has to be a jnana-yogi as well. Krishna places a very high value on knowledge that crystallizes into wisdom. But knowledge is not complete, or desirable, without shraddha, faith, spontaneous feeling, which in its best form becomes bhakti or devotion. Arjuna must learn to be a bhakti-yogi also.*

So, in the concluding Canto, the paths of action, knowledge and devotion merge in a single direction: moksha-samnyasa (which means salvation through self-surrender, or renunciation, and which is the title of the Canto).

'Act one must', says Krishna (shloka 11), but act only after learning from Sankhya philosophy that 'work is ruled by five causes: matter, agent, motive, motion, fate'. And, finally, 'have faith in me: worship me' (madbhakto mam namaskuru). That is the secret, for that enables a person to discover true self-dharma: 'One's own dharma, however imperfect, is a safer guide than the dharma of another, however perfect' (47).

The key shloka, the final advice, is in number 63: 'This is the subtle wisdom I give you. Think it over. You are free to choose' (yathecchasi tatha kuru). If the ultimate goal is freedom, the means too must be freedom to choose. 'Him whom I love, I would make free even from me.'

अर्जुन उवाच

संन्यासस्य महाबाहो तत्त्वमिच्छामि वेदितुम् ।
त्यागस्य च हृषीकेश पृथक्केशिनिषूदन ॥ १ ॥

श्रीभगवानुवाच

काम्यानां कर्मणां न्यासं संन्यासं कवयो विदुः ।
सर्वकर्मफलत्यागं प्राहुस्त्यां विचक्षणाः ॥ २ ॥

त्याज्यं दोषवदित्येके कर्म प्रहुर्मनीषिणः ।
यज्ञदानतपःकर्म न त्याज्यमिति चापरे ॥ ३ ॥

निश्चयं शृणु मे तत्र त्यागे भरतसत्तम ।
त्यागो हि पुरुषव्याघ्र त्रिविधाः संप्रकीर्तितः ॥ ४ ॥

यज्ञदानतपःकर्म न त्याज्यं कार्यमेव तत् ।
यज्ञो दानं तपश्चैव पावनानि मनीषिणाम् ॥ ५ ॥

एतान्यपि तु कर्माणि सङ्गं त्यक्त्वा फलानि च ।
कर्तव्यानीति मे पार्थ निश्चितं मतमुत्तमम् ॥ ६ ॥

नियतस्य तु संन्यासः कर्मणो नोपपद्यते ।
मोहात्तस्य परित्यागस्तामसः परिकीर्तितः ॥ ७ ॥

दुःखमित्येव यत्कर्म कायक्लेशभयात्त्यजेत् ।
स कृत्वा राजसं त्यां नैव त्यागफलं लभेत् ॥ ८ ॥

कार्यमित्येव यत्कर्म नियतं क्रियतेऽर्जुन ।
सङ्गं त्यक्त्वा फलं चैव स त्यागः सात्त्विको मतः ॥ ९ ॥

न द्वेष्ट्यकुशलं कर्म कुशले नानुषज्जते ।
त्यागी सत्त्वसमाविष्टो मेधावी छिन्नसंशयः ॥ १० ॥

न हि देहभृता शक्यं त्युक्तं कर्माण्यशेषतः ।
यस्तु कर्मफलत्यागी स त्यागीत्यभिधीयते ॥ ११ ॥

अनिष्टमिष्टं मिश्रं च त्रिविधं कर्मणः फलम् ।
भवत्यत्यागिनां प्रेत्य न तु संन्यासिनां क्वचित् ॥ १२ ॥

1   Arjuna said:
    Tell me, Krishna,
    the truth about renunciation, and about self-surrender.

2   Krishna replied:
    Renunciation means the giving-up of desire-laden action;
    self-surrender means giving up fruits of action.

3   Some thinkers say all work should be renounced;
    others prefer not to renounce rituals, charity, and tapasya.

4   But let me tell you what I think —
    giving-up is of three kinds.

5   Rituals, charity and tapasya should not be given up.
    They purify their performer.

6   But their fruits must always be given up.
    That is absolute.

7   Duties should not be given up.
    Only the tamasika give up duties.

8   Nor should fear of pain and injury be reason for giving up
    (as the rajasika do).

9   Duties performed without attachment or hope of reward
    are known as sattvika work.

10 The true renouncer, whose doubts have been dispelled,
    neither likes pleasant duty nor dislikes an unpleasant one.

11 Act one *must* —the body compels it —
    true giving-up is renunciation of fruits.

12 Action brings either pleasant, unpleasant, or mixed fruits
        after death.
    The true renouncer escapes them, the reward-seeker does
        not.

पञ्चैतानि महाबाहो कारणानि निबोध मे ।
सांख्ये कृतान्ते प्रोक्तानि सिद्धये सर्वकर्मणाम् ॥ १३ ॥

अधिष्ठानं तथा कर्ता करणं च पृथग्विधम् ।
विविधाश्च पृथक्चेष्टा दैवं चैवात्र पञ्चमम् ॥ १४ ॥

शरीरवाङ्मनोभिर्यत्कर्म प्रारभते नरः ।
न्याय्यं वा विपरीतं वा पञ्चैते तस्य हेतवः ॥ १५ ॥

तत्रैवं सति कर्तारमात्मानं केवलं तु यः ।
पश्यत्यकृतबुद्धित्वान्न स पश्यति दुर्मतिः ॥ १६ ॥

यस्य नाहंकृतो भावो बुद्धिर्यस्य न लिप्यते ।
हत्वापि स इमाँल्लोकान्न हन्ति न निबध्यते ॥ १७ ॥

ज्ञानं ज्ञेयं परिज्ञाता त्रिविधा कर्मचोदना ।
करणं कर्म कर्तेति त्रिविधः कर्मसंग्रहः ॥ १८ ॥

ज्ञानं कर्म च कर्ता च त्रिधैव गुणभेदतः ।
प्रोच्यते गुणसंख्याने यथावच्छृणु तान्यपि ॥ १९ ॥

सर्वभूतेषु येनैकं भावमव्ययमीक्षते ।
अविभक्तं विभक्तेषु तज्ज्ञानं विद्धि सात्त्विकम् ॥ २० ॥

पृथक्त्वेन तु यज्ज्ञानं नानाभावान्पृथग्विधान् ।
वेत्ति सर्वेषु भूतेषु तज्ज्ञानं विद्धि राजसम् ॥ २१ ॥

यत्तु कृत्स्नवदेकस्मिन्कार्ये सक्तमहेतुकम् ।
अतत्त्वार्थवदल्पं च तत्तामसमुदाहृतम् ॥ २२ ॥

नियतं सङ्गरहितमरागद्वेषतः कृतम् ।
अफलप्रेप्सुना कर्म यत्तत्सात्त्विकमुच्यते ॥ २३ ॥

यत्तु कामेप्सुना कर्म साहंकारेण वा पुनः ।
क्रियते बहुलायासं तद्राजसमुदाहृतम् ॥ २४ ॥

13   Learn from me Samkhya philosophy.
     All work is ruled by five causes —

14   Matter, agent,
     motive, motion, fate.

15   These five govern body, speech, and mind,
     whether right or wrong.

16   That is why the man who thinks the atman alone is the
          agent
     is blind —he sees nothing.

17   But the man who transcends his ego —though he destroys
          the worlds;
     destroys nothing —for he is not tainted by his action.

18   Knowledge, known and knower are the causes of action.
     Instrument, object and agent are the nexus of action.

19   Knowledge, action, agent are of three kinds, says Samkhya.
     Let me explain them to you.

20   Knowledge that sees Brahman everywhere, the one in the
          many,
     is sattvika.

21   Knowledge which sees difference everywhere,
          everywhere variety,
     is rajasika.

22   And that which sees only lies, pettiness and disunity,
     is tamasika.

23   Action performed without love or hate, without desire for
          its fruit,
     is sattvika.

24   Action performed with desire, pride, and struggle,
     is rajasika.

नुबन्धं क्षयं हिंसामनवेक्ष्य च पौरुषम् ।
मोहादारभ्यते कर्म यत्तत्तामसमुच्यते ॥ २५ ॥

मुक्तसङ्गोऽनहंवादी धृत्युत्साहसमन्वितः ।
सिद्ध्यसिद्ध्योर्निर्विकारः कर्ता सात्त्विक उच्यते ॥ २६ ॥

रागी कर्मफलप्रेप्सुर्लुब्धो हिंसात्मकोऽशुचिः ।
हर्षशोकान्वितः कर्ता राजसः परिकीर्तितः ॥ २७ ॥

अयुक्तः प्राकृतः स्तब्धः शठोऽनैष्कृतिकोऽलसः ।
विषादी दीर्घसूत्री च कर्ता तामस उच्यते ॥ २८ ॥

बुद्धेर्भेदं धृतेश्चैव गुणतस्त्रिविधं शृणु ।
प्रोच्यमानमशेषेण पृथक्त्वेन धनञ्जय ॥ २९ ॥

प्रवृत्तिं च निवृत्तिं च कार्याकार्ये भयाभये ।
बन्धं मोक्षं च या वेत्ति बुद्धिः सा पार्थ सात्त्विकी ॥ ३० ॥

यया धर्ममधर्मं च कार्यं चाकार्यमेव च ।
अयथावत्प्रजानाति बुद्धिः सा पार्थ राजसी ॥ ३१ ॥

अधर्मं धर्ममिति या मन्यते तमसावृता ।
सर्वार्थान्विपरीतांश्च बुद्धिः सा पार्थ तामसी ॥ ३२ ॥

धृत्या यया धारयते मनःप्राणेन्द्रियक्रियाः ।
योगेनाव्यभिचारिण्या धृतिः सा पार्थ सात्त्विकी ॥ ३३ ॥

यया तु धर्मकामार्थान्धृत्या धारयतेऽर्जुन ।
प्रसङ्गेन फलाकाङ्क्षी धृतिः सा पार्थ राजसी ॥ ३४ ॥

यया स्वप्नं भयं शोकं विषादं मदमेव च ।
न विमुञ्चति दुर्मेधा धृतिः सा पार्थ तामसी ॥ ३५ ॥

25   Action performed blindly, foolishly, and ruinously,
      is tamasika.

26   An agent free from attachment, unaffected by success or
         failure,
      is sattvika.

27   An agent who is passionate, ambitious and temperamental,
      is rajasika.

28   An agent unsteady, boorish, arrogant, dishonest, malicious,
         lazy, and despondent,
      is tamasika.

29   The mind is of three types too; so is discipline —
      let me explain.

30   The mind that knows the difference between what should
         be done and what should not be done,
         between right and wrong, bondage and liberation, fear
         and fearlessness,
      is sattvika.

31   The mind that is muddled on the meaning of dharma and
         adharma
      is rajasika.

32   The dark mind that thinks vice is virtue, adharma is dharma,
      is tamasika.

33   The discipline that organizes the mind, the life-breath, and
         the senses,
      is sattvika.

34   The discipline that leads to wealth, success, and honour,
      is rajasika.

35   And that which breeds sloth, fear, grief, worry, and conceit,
      is tamasika.

सुखं त्विदानीं त्रिविधं शृणु मे भरतर्षभ ।
अभ्यासाद्रमते यत्र दुःखान्तं च निगच्छति ॥ ३६ ॥

यत्तदग्रे विषमिव परिणामेऽमृतोपमम् ।
तत्सुखं सात्त्विकं प्रोक्तमात्मबुद्धिप्रसादजम् ॥ ३७ ॥

विषयेन्द्रियसंयोगाद्यत्तदग्रेऽमृतोपमम् ।
परिणामे विषमिव तत्सुखं राजसं स्मृतम् ॥ ३८ ॥

यदग्रे चानुबन्धे च सुखं मोहनमात्मनः ।
निद्रालस्यप्रमादोत्थं तत्तामसमुदाहृतम् ॥ ३९ ॥

न तदस्ति पृथिव्यां वा दिवि देवेषु वा पुनः ।
सत्त्वं प्रकृतिजैर्मुक्तं यदेभिः सयात्त्रिभिर्गुणैः ॥ ४० ॥

ब्राह्मणक्षत्रियविशां शूद्राणां च परंतप ।
कर्माणि प्रविभक्तानि स्वभावप्रभवैर्गुणैः ॥ ४१ ॥

शमो दमस्तपः शौचं क्षान्तिरार्जवमेव च ।
ज्ञानं विज्ञानमास्तिक्यं ब्रह्मकर्म स्वभावजम् ॥ ४२ ॥

शौर्यं तेजो धृतिर्दाक्ष्यं युद्धे चाप्यपलायनम् ।
दानमीश्वरभावश्च क्षात्रं कर्म स्वभावजम् ॥ ४३ ॥

कृषिगौरक्ष्यवाणिज्यं वैश्यकर्म स्वभावजम् ।
परिचर्यात्मकं कर्म शूद्रस्यापि स्वभावजम् ॥ ४४ ॥

स्वे स्वे कर्मण्यभिरतः संसिद्धिं लभते नरः ।
स्वकर्मनिरतः सिद्धिं यथा विन्दति तच्छृणु ॥ ४५ ॥

यतः प्रवृत्तिर्भूतानां येन सर्वमिदं ततम् ।
स्वकर्मणा तमभ्यर्च्य सिद्धिं विन्दति मानवः ॥ ४६ ॥

श्रेयान्स्वधर्मो विगुणः परधर्मात्स्वनुष्ठितात् ।
स्वभावनियतं कर्म कुर्वन्नाप्नोति किल्बिषम् ॥ ४७ ॥

36 There are three types of joys.
    The joy which is first poison but in the end nectar,

37 The joy enjoyed almost as a habit by the transparent mind,
    is sattvika.

38 The joy of sense pleasures, first nectar, then poison,
    is rajasika.

39 The joy of self-delusion, bred by sloth and folly,
    is tamasika.

40 There is nothing on earth, nothing in heaven,
    that is not the product of the three gunas.

41 Then there are the four castes, with their different duties —
    the Brahmins, Kshatriyas, Vaishyas, and Shudras.

42 Duties for the Brahmin:
    control of the mind and senses, patience, honesty,
        knowledge, and belief in an after-life.

43 Duties for the Kshatriya:
    courage, bravery, cleverness, fearlessness, generosity,
        and knowing how to rule a kingdom,

44 Duties for the Vaishya:
    tilling the land, cattle-rearing, and trade.
        For the Shudra: service.

45 Each following his conscientious duty, each finds perfection.
    Let me explain how this happens.

46 Perfection is achieved
    when a man dedicates his work to Brahman whose breath
        is the universe.

47 One's own dharma, however imperfect, is a safer guide
        than the dharma of another, however perfect.
    Conscience is what matters.

सहजं कर्म कौन्तेय सदोषमपि न त्यजेत् ।
सर्वारम्भा हि दोषेण धूमेनाग्निरिवावृताः ॥ ४८ ॥

असक्तबुद्धिः सर्वत्र जितात्मा विगतस्पृहः ।
नैष्कर्म्यसिद्धिं परमां संन्यासेनाधिगच्छति ॥ ४९ ॥

सिद्धिं प्राप्तो यथा ब्रह्म तथाप्नोति निबोध मे ।
समासेनैव कौन्तेय निष्ठा ज्ञानस्य या परा ॥ ५० ॥

बुद्ध्या विशुद्धया युक्तो धृत्यात्मानं नियम्य च ।
शब्दादीन्विषयांस्त्यक्त्वा रागद्वेषौ व्युदस्य च ॥ ५१ ॥

विविक्तसेवी लध्वाशी यतवाक्कायमानसः ।
ध्यानयोगपरो नित्यं वैराग्यं समुपाश्रितः ॥ ५२ ॥

अहङ्कारं बलं दर्पं कामं क्रोधं परिग्रहम् ।
विमुच्य निर्ममः शान्तो ब्रह्मभूयाय कल्पते ॥ ५३ ॥

ब्रह्मभूतः प्रसन्नात्मा न शोचति न काङ्क्षति ।
समः सर्वेषु भूतेषु मद्भक्तिं लभते पराम् ॥ ५४ ॥

भक्त्या मामभिजानाति यावान्यश्चास्मि तत्त्वतः ।
ततो मां तत्त्वतो ज्ञात्वा विशते तदनन्तरम् ॥ ५५ ॥

सर्वकर्माण्यपि सदा कुर्वाणो मद्व्यपाश्रयः ।
मत्प्रसादादवाप्नोति शाश्वतं पदमव्ययम् ॥ ५६ ॥

चेतसा सर्वकर्माणि मयि संन्यस्य मत्परः ।
बुद्धियोगमुपाश्रित्य मच्चित्तः सततं भव ॥ ५७ ॥

मच्चित्तः सर्वदुर्गाणि मत्प्रसादात्तरिष्यसि ।
अथ चेत्त्वमहंकारान्न श्रोष्यसि विनङ्क्ष्यसि ॥ ५८ ॥

यदहङ्कारमाश्रित्य न योत्स्य इति मन्यसे ।
मिथ्यैष व्यवसायस्ते प्रकृतिस्त्वां नियोक्ष्यति ॥ ५९ ॥

48   Follow your duty, Arjuna, as your nature dictates it.
     All work fetters, as all fire gives smoke. Only selfless duty
        saves.

49   Detachment, discipline, desirelessness, renunciation —
     these bring true freedom.

50   Let me tell you briefly how Brahman is achieved,
     Brahman, the end of all knowledge.

51   When the mind is pure and the intellect subdued,
     when love and hate no longer affect a person;

52   A lonely spot is sought, little is eaten, meditation is
        practised,
     the ego surrendered;

53   'I' and 'mine' disappear, peace is attained.
     These are the preconditions for achieving Brahman.

54   Once Brahman is achieved, there is no more sorrow, no
        more desire,
     there is only serenity.

55   Then does the yogi really know my nature, what and who
        I am.
     He knows me, and becomes me.

56   And though he works, my grace makes him free.
     He works in the shadow of my grace.

57   Fix your mind on me, Arjuna.
     Surrender all deeds to me.

58   All problems will be solved by my grace.
     Selfishness can lead only to your moral ruin.

59   If, filled with pride, you say, 'I will not fight,'
        it is all in vain, you are foolish.
     Fight you will, your nature will make you fight.

स्वभावजेन कौन्तेय निबद्धः स्वेन कर्मणा ।
कर्तुं नेच्छसि यन्मोहात्करिष्यस्यवशोऽपि तत् ॥ ६० ॥

ईश्वरः सर्वभूतानां हृद्देशेऽर्जुन तिष्ठति ।
भ्रामयन्सर्वभूतानि यन्त्रारूढानि मायया ॥ ६१ ॥

तमेव शरणं गच्छ सर्वभावेन भारत ।
तत्प्रसादात्परां शान्तिं स्थानं प्राप्स्यसि शाश्वतम् ॥ ६२ ॥

इति ते ज्ञानमाख्यातं गुह्याद्गुह्यतरं मया ।
विमृश्यैतदशेषेण यथेच्छसि तथा कुरु ॥ ६३ ॥

सर्वगुह्यतमं भूयः शृणु मे परमं वचः ।
इष्टोऽसि मे दृढमिति ततो वक्ष्यामि ते हितम् ॥ ६४ ॥

मन्मना भव मद्भक्तो मद्याजी मां नमस्कुरु ।
मामेवैष्यसि सत्यं ते प्रतिजाने प्रियोऽसि मे ॥ ६५ ॥

सर्वधर्मान्परित्यज्य मामेकं शरणं व्रज ।
अहं त्वा सर्वपापेभ्यो मोक्षयिष्यामि मा शुचः ॥ ६६ ॥

इदं ते नातपस्काय नाभक्ताय कदाचन ।
न चाशुश्रूषवे वाच्यं न च मां योऽभ्यसूयति ॥ ६७ ॥

य इमं परमं गुह्यं मद्भक्तेष्वभिधास्यति ।
भक्तिं मयि परां कृत्वा मामेवैष्यत्यसंशयः ॥ ६८ ॥

न च तस्मान्मनुष्येषु कश्चिन्मे प्रियकृत्तमः ।
भविता न च मे तस्मादन्यः प्रियतरो भुवि ॥ ६९ ॥

अध्येष्यते च य इमं धर्म्यं संवादमावयोः ।
ज्ञानयज्ञेन तेनाहमिष्टः स्यामिति मे मतिः ॥ ७० ॥

श्रद्धावाननसूयश्च शृणुयादपि यो नरः ।
सोऽपि मुक्तः शुभाँल्लोकान्प्राप्नुयात्पुण्यकर्मणाम् ॥ ७१ ॥

60 Your karma will make you fight.
    You are foolish. You will fight in spite of yourself.

61 Doesn't the world revolve like a magic wheel?
    Isn't Brahman the hub of the heart?

62 Take shelter in him, and find peace.
    His grace will give you eternal peace.

63 This is the subtle wisdom I give you.
    Think it over. You are free to choose.

64 I tell you all this because I love you.
    Listen to this subtle wisdom.

65 Think only of me. Have faith in me. Worship me.
        You cannot fail to find me.
    I love you, so I promise you this.

66 Throw away your dharmas —
        have faith in me, take refuge in me.
    And do not fear —you will be saved.

67 And never repeat this wisdom to the cynical, the sensual,
    the blasphemous and faithless.

68 The devoted teacher of this wisdom
    to faithful listeners will always come to me.

69 What sweeter service can there be than his?
    None is dearer to me than he.

70 Whoever reads this dialogue of dharma offers me his
        knowledge.
    This is my belief.

71 Even the devoted listener will find the heaven where good
        men go.
    He too shall be saved.

कच्चिदेतच्छुतं पार्थ त्वयैकाग्रेण चेतसा ।
कच्चिदज्ञानसंमोहः प्रनष्टस्ते धनञ्जय ॥ ७२ ॥

अर्जुन उवाच

नष्टो मोहः स्मृतिर्लब्धा त्वत्प्रसादान्मयाच्युत ।
स्थितोऽस्मि गतसन्देहः करिष्ये वचनं तव ॥ ७३ ॥

सञ्जय उवाच

इत्यहं वासुदेवस्य पार्थस्य च महात्मनः ।
संवादमिममश्रौषमद्भुतं रोमहर्षणम् ॥ ७४ ॥

व्यासप्रसादाच्छुतवानेतद्गुह्यमहं परम् ।
योगं योगेश्वरात्कृष्णात्साक्षात्कथयतः स्वयम् ॥ ७५ ॥

राजन्संसृत्य संसृत्य संवादमिममद्भुतम् ।
केशवार्जुनयोः पुण्यं हृष्यामि च मुहुर्मुहुः ॥ ७६ ॥

तच्च संसृत्य संसृत्य रूपमत्यद्भुतं हरेः ।
विस्मयो मे महान् राजन् हृष्यामि च पुनः पुनः ॥ ७७ ॥

यत्र योगेश्वरः कृष्णो यत्र पार्थो धनुर्धरः ।
तत्र श्रीर्विजयो भूतिर्ध्रुवा नीतिर्मतिर्मम ॥ ७८ ॥

72   Have you listened carefully, Arjuna?
      Is your ignorance gone? Are your doubts dispelled?

73   Arjuna replied:
      My doubts are gone, Krishna, thanks to your grace.
      I am not confused. I will do as you say.

74   Sanjaya reported:
      I heard this wonderful dialogue between Krishna and
          mahatma Arjuna,
      and I horripilated.

75   By the grace of Vyasa did I hear this subtle wisdom, this
          yoga,
      straight from the lips of Krishna.

76   Your majesty, every time I recall this holy dialogue between
          Krishna and Arjuna,
      I am thrilled, joy overcomes me.

77   Every time I recall Krishna's marvellous Multi-Revelation,
      I am wonderstruck —joy overcomes me.

78   Where Krishna, lord of yoga, is,
      where Arjuna, wielder of the bow, is,
      are victory, success, prosperity, and law.
      I am convinced of this.